THE BLUEPRINT TO INTELLIGENT INVESTORS

VOLUME 2

STOCK AND SHARES TRADING, HOW TO BECOME A MILLIONAIRE AND PRIVATE PLACEMENT PROGRAMS

SIR PATRICK BIJOU

DESCRIPTION

Discover the Blueprint to Intelligent Investing and Follow the Smart Way to Increase Your Wealth!

Dear reader,

Do you know what the sad truth about the world is? Well, the fact that the odds are most often against you. And do you know what's even more painful? That there is a way to turn those odds in your favor, but people are afraid to start using that!

Discover the easy way to secure financially yourself, your children, and their children for a lifetime with foolproof investing principles.

This is not one of those books that will show you how to "get rich quick" or "become famous and make it"! What this book will show you is the blueprint to turning the odds into your favor - blueprint to intelligent investing - blueprint to happiness. It will show you how to stop being a slave to money and instead make money work for you.

How to turn the odds into your favor and level the playing field? With smart investing, of course.

Too many books on stocks are as thick as college textbooks and not nearly as exciting. With this book in your hands, you won't have to wade through hundreds of pages and dozens of books to actually learn something valuable. Everything you need to know to start investing can be found inside.

Here is what this skilfully crafted guide can offer you:

- Blueprint to intelligent investing
- Smart investing strategies that always work
- Guide to make your money work for you
- Way to gain financial stability and independence
- Everything you need to know about the investing market - the players, the rules, and the vocabulary
- And much more!

If you want to turn your wage into a fortune and make your money work for you, all you have to do is to follow foolproof guides and expert advice found in this book. So what are you waiting for?

ABOUT THE AUTHOR

Like never before, the accomplishment of a business relies upon how well you draw with clients and construct positive encounters. This at last results in a solid brand dependability. Sir Patrick is a dynamic investment banker, Fund Manager, and REDEMPTION JUDGE for the International Court of Justice and International Criminal Courts, he is also Ambassador for WORLD PEACE TRACTS and a published Author.

As a notable investment banker, he has also worked on Wall Street, a very capable and highly experienced trader in the derivative and bond markets, having setup MTN desks within Lloyds Bank. Sir Patrick's journey into content writing has allowed him to become an exceptionally motivated and enthusiastic author and professional communicator. Experienced in both proactive campaign-driven and responsive communications.

He has been responsible for serving large corporates, the creation of new credit for international supply chains and SMEs, public sector, and clients across a range of products that include supply chain finance, receivable finance, contract monetization and a broad range of trade services. Sir Patrick undertook similar roles at Conduit Capital and

Morgan Stanley. His extensive contacts are with major banks around the world and include Wells Fargo, HSBC, and BNP Paribas where he deals at board level. Today, he determines it is right to take this concept to the next level and help others free their full business potential.

Sir Patrick has tailored funding and investments for many different clients including governments, banks and financial institutions, and has implemented over $1.3B funding for social housing.

Coming together is a beginning, keeping together is progress, and working together is a success"

Thank you for reading this book and please write a review.

TABLE OF CONTENTS

INTRODUCTION

This book was compiled to demonstrate that it is possible to invest in the shares of UK- quoted companies in a sensible and logical manner that requires no special expertise; also, that the results will, in the long term, be better than those of more than half of the highly-paid professional fund managers.

It is directed at readers who may be considering investment on the Stockmarket as part of a balanced portfolio of investments. The early sections review features of the Stockmarket in a manner which is illustrative rather than definitive, showing the reasons underlying a 'logical investment strategy'.

The first chapter provides an overview of the whole book, and should be read first. Subsequent chapters look more closely at the features of share investment and examine various strategies for investment on the Stockmarket with special emphasis on the 'logical investment strategy'.

The closing chapters deal with additional areas for investment likely to appeal to the more experienced private investor, such as traded options, gilts, and bonds.

It is hoped that this book will serve the reader not only as a general investment guide but also as a handy reference manual to be kept on the bookshelf. Numerous technical terms are explained at length and a substantial glossary has also been provided.

It is most important for the reader to remember one central tenet

- past performance is no guide to future performance. That means that the logical investment strategy cannot be guaranteed to work in the future.

CHAPTER 1

The Art Of Dividend Investing

I am not a therapist, and this book is not a journey into navel gazing and self-discovery. That being said, you have to get this part right.

Investor psychology and sentiment play a significant role in how you approach investments and the investing process. In my experience the most successful investors have had an end goal in mind that they wanted to achieve, which necessarily dictated the majority of their investment decisions. This is not to say that you can't be a successful investor without having a game plan mapped out, but understanding your motivation for putting your hard-earned money at risk in the markets can help you avoid taking unnecessary risks.

With that in mind, forgive my waxing philosophical for a moment. If September 11, 2001 has taught us anything, let's hope it's that life is precious and time is valuable. If you accept this premise as true, you would agree with me, then, that ideally, we should spend as much time as possible in this life to find and embrace our passions;

those activities that make our hearts swell and our souls soar.

The reality though is that we don't live in an ideal world. As human beings we have to spend a significant portion of our time providing for the practical necessities: food, clothing, housing, transportation, education, recreation, and medication. The means by which we acquire these necessities is called cash.

It's All About the Cash

Generating sufficient cash to meet your needs will be a primary objective until you die. If you have loved ones you are responsible for, they will continue to need cash after you die.

During the employment years, you must make wages, salaries, and bonuses do double duty, providing for current needs while investing for the future. Optimally, the invested cash will generate sufficient interest, dividends, and capital appreciation to meet your future needs when your wages, salaries, and bonuses are no longer your primary sources of income. Your long-term challenge then will be to balance your cashflow between your current cash needs and your need to accumulate cash for the future. Your level of success in this endeavor can be positively impacted by a modicum of financial planning.

Financial planning is an excellent exercise and a useful tool to organize your financial activities and to create a disciplined structure. Although some practitioners can overwhelm you with the minutia, an understanding of your current cashflow and budget is sufficient to make some reasonable assumptions for a retirement budget. This information will provide a working framework for how much you need to save, the required rate of return on those savings to meet your goals, and how much insurance you need to protect yourself and your loved ones should you become disabled or die prematurely. Armed with that information and this book, you can accomplish the rest.

Technology has changed the world, our culture, and social mores. This new era of interconnectivity has accelerated the pace at which we receive information and process its applicability to our lives. By extension, the workplace and the work ethic have evolved as well. The time when one would choose a career track with one employer or within one industry from beginning to end has vanished. Second, third, and even fourth careers are now commonplace. Again, by extension, retirement or at least the concept of retirement has also evolved. The twentieth-century model of moving from employment to the golden years in pursuit of leisure has morphed into the reality that for many, whether by choice or necessity, a portion of the golden years now includes some form of continuing employment.

The recession and cyclical downturn in housing beginning in 2008 notwithstanding, the long-term economic reality is that historically the cost of living increases year after year. Unless your cashflow increases at the same rate as the cost of your expenditures, you will have to decide between spending on current needs and investing for future needs.

Barring a major depression or the end of the world, the cost of living and the average life span will most likely continue to increase. Assuming I am correct, you need to be prepared for the rising cost of the practical necessities for a greater amount of time. This is to say you are going to need a lot of cash. Granted, we all have unique circumstances and situations, so how we approach spending and investing will vary by the individual. Regardless of the myriad factors to consider, don't just stick your head in the sand and hope for the best; hope is not a strategy for success.

The Importance of Planning

As an investment advisor, I have witnessed too frequently the stress and anxiety of investors who have underestimated their cash needs for retirement. Because retirement planning didn't gain wide ac-ceptance until the early nineties, too many waited to properly fund their 401(k) plans, IRAs, and after-tax investments and savings, and/or they weren't properly invested. I can't tell you how many people have told me that they thought that Social Security would make up the difference. Although Social Security worked well when the demographics were more favorable, ensuring benefits for future recipients required changes in the system that were never instituted. Today we are faced with the prospect of a bankrupt program. Although there are voices that advocate long-needed reforms, I would suggest that there will not be any significant changes made to Social Security because it is politically too hot to handle. For the reader below 40 years of age this is unfortunate; I wouldn't count on Social Security being available to supplement your retirement. Let's all hope that I am very, very wrong.

Undoubtedly there are some readers who are proactive and better prepared, who embraced retirement planning early on by funding a 401(k), an IRA, and after-tax investments. By design or by luck, some will have invested well and will be on track; others won't be so lucky. If you are unsure about where you stand, don't guess. If you need help, engage a fee-based financial planner. Your tax preparer or attorney should have some ready references. Whether you go it alone or require some assistance, however, just make sure you get it done. Knowing what you need and when you will need it is critical to the investment process. When it comes to your future, don't be afraid to ask questions. In my experience, few people have the answers to these questions off the top of their heads. It isn't that they aren't capable, but most people prefer to concentrate on activities they find more attractive. I understand that perspective because most people naturally gravitate to what most interests them. Some of us are butchers, others are bakers, and many are candlestick makers. So I say again, don't guess; find out what you'll need so you get your goals and objectives in focus, and then we can help you with the rest.

If you know what your goals and objectives are, you are well on your way to achieving investment success. At the end of the day, successful investing is realized by three activities:know the end goal(s) of why you are investing; use an investment approach that makes sense to you and can generate returns sufficient to meet your goals; and, keep an eye on taxes and expenses. The three activities, shown in Figure 1.1, are nothing more than being mindful about your investments and investment decisions.

You put thought and consideration into other critical areas of your life, why shouldn't you do the same about your investments? Think of it this way: By entertaining some mindful decision-making about your investments, you just might eliminate any fears and anxiety you may have about your financial future.

How's that for a payoff?

As stated previously, little has changed in human nature. The two base emotions of fear and greed are still the most difficult challenges most investors face. The fear of losing money on a poor investment is equaled only by the fear of losing money on a lost opportunity; both are directly attributable to a lack of good information. Making mindful, long-term investment decisions is almost impossible without good information.

It is ironic that, in the Information Age, the average investor suffers from information deprivation. On a certain level this seems absurd, considering the number of investment newsletters, magazines, and periodicals in publication; the financial shows with which the radio waves are congested;, and the content of cable television, offering more content around the clock than anyone can possibly assimilate. Well, yes, all of these sources are readily available. But so, what? The answer lies not in how much information is available but in how much is important. The investing public doesn't suffer from a lack of information; they suffer from a lack of relevant information.

Our Purpose

As the editor of an investment newsletter I don't wish to come off as self-serving or hypocritical, but there are two critical elements to understand about this point: content and purpose. At Investment Quality Trends we produce all of our content internally for the purpose of helping the subscriber to make well-informed investment decisions. At inception we decided that to remain independent and completely objective we would accept no outside advertising. Therefore, our revenues are based solely on subscriptions. That fact necessitates that our content must fulfill subscribers' needs for information that results in good investment decisions and profits, which results in continued subscriptions.

By comparison, much of the mainstream financial media is big business beholden to shareholders who expect its company to generate big revenues. Like all publicly traded companies, the sole function is to generate a profit, just like any other business in America. The means by which big media produces its profits is by advertising revenues. Advertising revenues are based on the number of people the audience that medium reaches. To encourage people to read, listen to, or view their medium, they have to create interest and grab the audience's attention.

Unfortunately, the means by which the audience's interest is grabbed isn't necessarily useful information. And, when questionable information is distributed by sources that are thought to be highly knowledgeable and dependable, it only compounds the problem.

On the other hand the information that will work for the audience isn't always commercially attractive or appealing. So, in wanting to be entertained, much of the investing public gravitates toward information that is the equivalent of nutritionally empty fast food, and then they wonder why they are suffering from malnutrition. The tragedy is that with vast exposure comes the mantle of credibility, which, unfortunately, often fails to result in any meaningful, longterm success. It is unconscionable that important investing information can be displaced by ridiculous though entertaining discussions that are simply useless and can distract you from the basic purpose of investing: generating sufficient cash to meet your or someone else's current and future cash needs while limiting risk. In addition to publishing Investment Quality Trends, we eat our own cooking for our private capital and as portfolio managers at our sister company for endowments, foundations, and the private trust accounts of high-net-worth individuals. The proven methods found in this book assist us in making thoughtful decisions about how to invest and realize the financial goals and objectives of our clients. From experience we have learned to ignore the useless information created by the junk food peddlers because it simply doesn't work. This book will show you what does work and how to properly use it to your advantage.

As portfolio managers we are subject to stringent legal and regulatory requirements and are held to a higher standard of competence. If we fail to meet our fiduciary responsibility, we are subject to tremendous liability. Consequently, we and like-minded professionals seek out and take advantage of the best information available; so should you.

Similarly to big financial media, the retail platform of investment products and advice, although well meaning, is designed for mass consumption. In a one- size-fits-all environment, it is inevitable that the average investor will be exposed to risks of which they are not aware. This is not an indictment of any individual but of the culture, which is sales and transaction oriented, not performance oriented.

A Trusted Approach

The performance-oriented approach has three areas of focus: understand what you need so you can establish achievable goals; make investments with the highest probability for meeting those goals; and limit taxes and expenses. Repeated studies confirm that the decisions you make in these three areas will make the most impact on the success or failure of your investment plan. My experience is that if you adopt these methods into your mindful investment decision¬making process you will enjoy higher returns while reducing your risk and increasing your chances of reaching your goals.

The strategy behind our approach, the dividend-value strategy, is based on the Dividend-Yield Theory, a value-based approach to investing. The term value can mean different things to different people. To us, knowing what represents value is the key to investing in the stock market. Investing in a company when it offers good historic value dramatically reduces downside risk to investment principal while providing the maximum upside potential for capital gains and growth of dividends.

Rather than some arbitrary definition or metric, the Dividend- Yield Theory uses a stock's dividend yield as the primary measure of value. Obviously price is important, but price on its own, without some substantive context, is meaningless. Beyond price then, an investor must have a proven method to establish whether the price of a company under investment consideration offers sufficient return potential to justify taking a risk with his investment capital.

According to the Dividend-Yield Theory, the price of a stock is driven by its yield. We delve into this concept deeper in following chapters, but in the simplest of terms, a stock is most attractive when it offers a high dividend yield. As investors rush in to lock down the high yield, their buying pushes the price higher. Eventually the price reaches an area where the current yield is no longer attractive and buying stops. With no new buyers to push the stock price higher, inertia sets in and the price begins to decline. At this juncture the early buyers will begin to sell and lock in their profits. When later investors see their profits evaporating, they will also sell to salvage what they can of their profits and principal. Eventually, the selling will push the yield back up to an area where once again it is sufficient to attract new buying interest.

So rather than emphasize price alone or a company's sector, products, or other analytical factors, the dividend-value strategy uses dividend-yield patterns to make buying and selling decisions. By understanding the historical dividend yield pattern of a company, the investor is better informed about whether the stock offers much value, little value, or somewhere in between.

One last aside as we begin our journey together: I will try to avoid industry jargon wherever possible. The English language is broad enough to explain this method and the process in a way that the everyday noninvestment professional can understand. This should help to lift the veil of mystery and confusion to what is actually a relatively simple process.

The Case for Investing in Stocks

We all have practical living needs that generally must be purchased with cash. At some point, typically in retirement, you will need a pool of cash to supplement your other sources of income. Unless you are independently wealthy, hit the lottery, or inherit a fortune from Great Aunt Sally, your options for growing wealth are fairly limited; in short, you will have to invest. As with any major venture, those who begin with achieving a specific goal or outcome have a much greater chance for success. Investing is no different.

The biggest mistake investors make is committing hard-earned money to investments, with absolutely no idea of why they are making those investments. Some of you are no doubt saying to yourself, "This guy must be thick. People invest to make money!" Let's agree among ourselves that that is a given. Now let's drill down to the heart of the issue: Money for what; money for whom; and, money for when?

Investment Needs

These questions are important; the answers are critical to your success. Simply plunging half-cocked into the markets with only a nebulous concept of making as much money as possible is an invitation to disaster. Minimally, you need to know two things: how much and when. Knowing how much you will need and when you will need it will allow you to devise a strategy, not just any strategy but a personal strategy to meet your specific individual needs. Trust me, without this base level of understanding you will do one of two things: shoot for the moon by assuming more risk than necessary to reach your goals and objectives; or play it too close to the vest and fall short of your goals and objectives.

When it comes to needs, there is no one-size-fits-all. Every investor is an individual with unique needs and objectives. You may have more than one objective; you may even have to prioritize among competing objectives such as education, retirement, big- ticket purchases, or even possible elder or special needs care. These objectives could be near term, long term, or a combination of the two. Your objectives may also need to be approached separately because there may be different factors to consider. If you can clearly answer these questions you will be in a much stronger position to meet your needs.

Once you have the end in mind there is only one thing you need to understand about investing: The sole purpose of investing is to grow your capital and income base to meet a current or future cash need. If you believe you might not meet your cash goals and objectives you will panic and take unnecessary risks, which generally result in loss and disappointment. So in simple terms, investing is about meeting needs, not hitting the lottery.

Stocks, Bonds, or Cash?

An entire book can be written (indeed, many already exist) on this subject alone. For our purposes I want to keep this simple: For most investors the majority of their investments will be made in the three primary asset classes: stocks,fixed-income (bonds), and cash or cash equivalents.

Cash and cash equivalents (short-term instruments that can be liquidated quickly with little to no loss of principal) serve several purposes. One purpose is to provide liquidity to meet current obligations; another is to temporarily hold interest and dividends that are earmarked for reinvestment; lastly, cash is a short¬term, low- risk alternative to stocks and bonds during periods of extreme market volatility.

As an asset class, stocks can be divided into many subsets: domestic and international; growth and value; large-cap, mid-cap, small-cap; developed and emerging markets, and so forth. The same is true for fixed-income instruments: taxable; tax-exempt; Treasuries; government agencies; mortgage-backed; high-yield; international; emerging markets, and so forth.

In addition to the common asset classes just listed, the contemporary financial marketplace also consists of alternative asset classes such as hedge funds, private equity, venture capital, direct real estate, precious metals and gemstones, art and antiquities, and, of course, futures and options contracts on almost everything. The list can go on forever.

Perhaps this is part of the problem: The investment landscape has become so cluttered and sophisticated that investors have lost site of the basics. When distilled down to the most basic level, however, there are two primary choices for investment capital: to loan or to own.

In the simplest of terms, when you invest in a fixed-income instrument—a CD, a T-Bill, a T-Bond, a corporate bond, a municipal bond—whatever the case, you are making a loan of your capital to the issuer. For the right to use your capital, the issuer promises to pay you a fixed rate of interest over the agreed upon period of the loan and to return your capital, in whole, at the end of the loan period, otherwise known as maturity.

When an investor buys shares of stock, he buys part ownership of a corporation. The return on a stock investment comes in two forms: capital appreciation (an increase in share price) and dividends, which we will discuss in greater detail shortly. Unlike a fixed- income investment, common stocks pay nofixed rate of interest and offer no guarantees for the return of capital.

The asset allocation decision (the percentage of capital allocated to stocks, bonds, and cash in a portfolio) is one of the basic yet most often confusing decisions an investor must make. Generally, the role of stocks is to provide long-term total returns (a combination of price appreciation and dividends). The role of bonds is to provide an income stream.

When considering the respective risks and rewards of stocks versus fixed-income, stocks, in theory, have unlimited appreciation potential. That is, there is no upper limit on how high the price of a stock may go. A fixed-income investor, on the other hand, generally knows the maximum return potential for a fixed- income investment, especially if it is held to maturity. Although it is true that a fixed-income instrument can sell at a premium, prior to maturity, the potential for price appreciation is significantly lower than the potential for price appreciation in stocks.

This brings us to one of the major areas of disagreement among investors,financial academics, and the investment industry: What is risk? Before I address that question, a long-held tenet of investing is that risk goes hand-in-hand with reward: no risk, no reward. Based on your definition and understanding of risk, this may or may not be true.

My belief is that, if you ask the average investor (not a professional or academic) how they define risk, they would tell you it is the possibility of losing money on an investment, meaning a partial or total loss of the original investment principal. Financial academics— and the investment industry in general—define risk as the short-term (annual, monthly, or daily) volatility of returns. The volatility of returns is measured by variance or standard deviation; think fluctuation.

Without opening a huge can of worms, what is a loss? Is it a realized loss (selling an investment for less than the original outlay) or a paper loss (holding an investment with a current market value below the purchase price)? Don't laugh; you won't believe how people can get all tied up in knots over this.

For the short-term investor who may need the use of funds today, next week, or next month, there isn't much to argue here; any definition of loss means they have less money to work with and are feeling pain. For the long-term investor who has a 20-year time horizon, it might make strategic sense to take a quick realized loss on an investment gone awry because they have time to make up the difference and then some. On the other hand, if the investment is sound but just temporarily depressed (paper loss), why get shook up over short-term market fluctuations?

For the short-term investor, then, risk is not having sufficient liquid or near liquid funds to meet cash needs at the present and out To five years. If this applies to your situation, then you don't need to be anywhere near investments that can and will fluctuate significantly over the short-term, period.

As investment instruments, both stocks and bonds have apparent risks. Stocks may not have a theoretical ceiling, but they do have a bottom: Stocks can fall to zero and become worthless. With fixed- income investments, there is the possibility of a decline in the market value due to an increase in interest rates. There is also the possibility the issuer will be unable to make interest or principal payments on time or at all, effectively defaulting on the loan.

For the long-term investor, though,fixed-income investments have a whopper of a risk that is subtle to the eye yet very dangerous; that is, inflation risk. Inflation risk is the possibility that the stream of income payments and eventual return of principal will decline in purchasing power (not keep pace with inflation).

For the long-term investor, then, neither the average-investor definition nor the academic/industry definition adequately addresses risk. With regard to the average-investor definition, much of the risk can be mitigated through education about appropriate investment time horizons and limiting investment considerations to high-quality investments that offer historic good value.

With regard to the academic/industry definition of risk, short-term (annual or even less frequent) price fluctuations (volatility) aren't as relevant to the long¬term investor with a 20-year time horizon as is building sufficient long-term wealth to meet future cash needs. Secondly, this focus on volatility is almost always based on nominal returns, which ignores the loss of purchasing power caused by inflation.

For short-term investors inflation isn't such a big concern but for long-term investors the impact can be huge.

The Case for Stocks

As the editor of a stock investment newsletter and portfolio manager that specializes in blue chip stocks, I am obviously an advocate of investing in stocks. Let me tell you why.

Most investors are familiar with the concept of total return: capital gains (price appreciation) plus dividend yield. As a formula we would write it like this:

Capital gains dividend yield 1/4 total return

Let's use an example. You buy a stock for $25 per share and at the end of three years the price has increased to $50 per share. The capital gain is $25 per share or 100 percent. Let's assume the stock paid a $1 per share dividend the first year, a $1.10 dividend per share the next year, and $1.21 per share in dividends the third year. By adding the $3.31 in dividends to the $25 capital gain, the total gain equals $28.31.

To find the percentage return, we divide the total gain ($28.31) by the purchase price ($25), which is 113 percent. This represents the total return on investment for the three years. On a simple basis, the average annual return equals 37 percent per year.

The IQ Trends dividend-value strategy adds another component to the concept of total return, namely, dividend growth.

Capital gains dividend yield dividend growth 1/4 real total return The growth potential of real total return is the underlying reason and really, the only viable reason for investors to invest in stocks.

Although fixed-income investments offer a fixed return, it is only in a declining interest rate environment that fixed-income investments offer the potential for capital gains. Growth of dividends, however, is only achievable in the stock market. In later chapters we delve deeper into the importance of dividends and dividend growth to stock prices, but for now, know that only in the stock market can you achieve real total return.

In the final analysis, the true benefit of real total return is only understood when you consider the damage inflicted on capital by the twin evils of taxes and inflation. That is, if nothing is left to spend or reinvest after taxes and inflation, you have nothing to show for the risk you assumed. If you are putting your hard- earned money at risk, then shouldn't it be in the area with the highest probability of leaving you with something to show for your efforts?

The Growth Rates of Stocks

For the 83-year period from 1926-2008, the nominal, compound average rate of return for stocks (the S&P 500) was 9.60 percent. Twenty-year government bonds returned 5.70 percent and 30-day Treasury Bills 3.70 percent. Adjusting for a compound average rate of inflation at 3.0 percent, the real returns were 7.10 percent, 2.20 percent, and 0.50 percent, respectively.

After you factor in taxes, 30-day Treasury Bills are a virtual wash and 20-year Treasury Bonds are only slightly better. Only stocks have historically provided real, long-term growth of capital.

Now to be fair, nobody has an 83-year investment time horizon. There is also the argument that historical returns are irrelevant because those economic conditions are not applicable to today's— maybe, maybe not. What I know about the stock market though is that it takes everything into consideration: the past, present, and as a discounting mechanism, the future.

Without the benefit of clairvoyance, we have to look at what we do know, and that is the past. Although the past guarantees nothing, it does provide insight into how investments have performed under various economic conditions over varying time frames.

The common trap when looking at the past, however, is to cherry- pick the data that supports the thesis. Indeed, there is an entire body of investment theory that is based on torturing the data until it confesses; I won't be a party to that and you deserve better. That being said, it is reasonable to review holding periods that are representative of those of the average investor so we can find some commonality for returns.

Let's start with a very reasonable time-frame of 20 years as shown in Figure 2.1. In the 64 rolling 20-year holding periods from 1926 through 2008, stocks (the S&P 500) out performed fixed-income (20- year government bonds) in each instance except two: the 20 years from 1929-1948 and 1989-2008. Let's put that into perspective: Stocks outperformed bonds in 62 of 64 20-year periods, or 96.8 percent of the time.

That is a pretty high batting average, which almost begs the question of what happened in the two periods when stocks under performed bonds. For the period beginning in 1929 the answer is fairly simple—the Great Crash of 1929. By the time it ended in 1932, stocks had declined by almost 90 percent. It takes a while to dig out of a hole that deep.

For the 20-year period beginning in 1989 the story is a little different. Instead of stock prices declining at the beginning of the period, as in 1929-1932, the declines came at the end of the period: 2000-2002 and October 2007 through the end of 2008.

Per the norm, analysts and economists disagree about the reasons for the declines in these two periods. In the final analysis, the only opinion that matters is that of the investors who did the buying and selling. In both periods, however, there is a strong argument that valuations were excessive. From 1926 through 1928 stocks increased by 120.40 percent on a nominal basis, a simple average annual return of 40 percent per year. From 1989-1999 stocks increased by 221.40 percent on a nominal basis, a simple

Total Return

average annual return of 20.12 percent per year. A 20 percent return in any given year is not out of the ordinary—to average that for 11 consecutive years, however, is extraordinary. We deal with values and valuations thoroughly in later chapters, but there was some commonality in the two periods. The dividend- yield for the Dow Jones Industrial Average was at historically repetitive areas of overvalue. Understanding the connection between dividend-yield and values will help you to avoid periods of overvaluation both in individual stocks and in the broad market.

That bonds outperformed in these two periods is also easy to understand; both were periods of declining interest rates, when bonds tend to enjoy price premiums. With current bond yields at or near historic lows and stocks having corrected significantly, you have to consider which asset class offers the greater potential moving forward.

If 20 years strikes you as too long a period, Figure 2.2 shows that in the 74 rolling 10-year holding periods from 1926-2008, stocks (the S&P 500) outperformed fixed-income (20-year government bonds) in 64 periods or 86 percent of the time. What is immediately apparent is that, when the holding period decreases (20 years to 10 years) the percentage of time that stocks outperformed bonds also decreases, which lends support to the argument that the longer the holding period the greater probability stocks will out-perform bonds.

Once again, 86 percent is a pretty high batting average. As we did with the 20-year periods above, what can we learn by looking at the 10 periods when stocks underperformed bonds? The first four 10- year rolling periods were the ones that ended in 1937, 1938, 1939 and 1940. Obviously these periods were impacted by the Great Crash. The next three

10-year rolling periods are also interrelated: 1974, 1977 and 1978. These three rolling periods encompassed much of the bear market that ran from 1966 through year-end 1974.

In 2000 one of the longest bull market runs in history came to an end with the tech and dot-com meltdowns. The declines over the three years between 2000 and year-end 2002 were so severe that the 10-year rolling period ending in 2002 became the eighth 10-year rolling period of 10 where stocks underperformed bonds. The last two rolling 10-year periods should come as no surprise: 2007 and 2008. As the bear sank his teeth into the markets much of the gains from the latter part of the 1990s were washed away in a sea of red.

Total Return

What should be obvious at this point is that any period when a bear market is in force necessarily results in a period of under- performance for stocks. As noted previously, much of this can be avoided through an understanding of values and valuations.

The final segments of returns we will review are shown in Figure 2.3 and review the 79 rolling 5-year periods from 1926- 2008. Stocks (the S&P 500) out performed fixed-income (20-year government bonds) in 58 of 79 periods or 73.41 percent of the time. Once again we see that when the holding period decreases (10 years to 5 years) the percentage of time that stocks outperformed bonds also decreases.

Although the percentage of periods when stocks outperformed bonds decreases when the number of years in the holding period decreases, 73 percent is still a relatively high number. As we found with the returns for the rolling holding periods for 10 and 20 years, the returns for the 5-year rolling periods when stocks underperformed bonds consisted wholly or in part of years that fell within a bear market.

Knowing investor psychology the way I do, some of you are undoubtedly thinking "73.41 percent is darn near three out of four; those are odds I can live with. May be five years is a sufficient holding period for stocks."

Ultimately you will have to make that call. Before you do, though, consider this: On a real return basis, stocks have had four calendar year losses of over 30 percent in the 83 years from 1926-2008. In two of the four instances, 1931 and 1974, the calendar year preceding each also recorded losses. In these two instances the consecutive calendar year losses totaled over 50 percent. There's simply no way to put lipstick on that pig. If two of the five years in your investment time horizon is that one out of four when stocks go south, you aren't going to think three out of four is so great. As I suggested previously, where the rubber really meets the road for the long-term investor is the real (after-inflation) return. As such, let's look at the 20-, 10-, and 5-year rolling holding periods after adjusting for inflation.

In the 64 rolling 20-year holding periods from 1926¬2008, stocks (the S&P 500) outperformed fixed- income (20-year government bonds) in each instance except one: the 20 years from 1989-2008. Sixty-three of 64 periods is 98.43 percent.

Total Return

The Case for Investing in Stocks In the 74 rolling 10-year holding periods from 1926¬2008, stocks (the S&P 500) outperformed fixed- income (20-year government bonds) in 63 periods or 85 percent of the time; that is one less period than on a nominal basis.

In the 79 rolling 5-year holding periods from 1926¬2008, stocks (the S&P 500) outperformed fixed- income (20-year government bonds) in 58 of the 79 periods or 73.41 percent of the time; these are identical to the results on a nominal basis.

Knowledge, Strategy, and Tactics

We have covered a lot of ground in this chapter, so let me summarize the most salient points. Inflation is a constant in our capital system. As such, the cost of the practical necessities will probably continue to increase over time. In the event you don't earn, inherit, or win a fortune, you will necessarily need to set aside and invest a portion of your capital to build a pool of cash and stream of income to meet your future needs.

The major risk for the short-term investor is a capital loss. The major risk for the long-term investor is inflation and insufficient capital growth.

Of the myriad asset classes available for investment, most of your investment decisions will be centered on the allocation of your investment capital into the three primary asset classes of stocks, bonds, and cash.

Bonds provide for a specific rate of return over a specified period and a return of investment principal upon maturity. With the exception of a period of declining interest rates, the potential for capital appreciation is minimal. The apparent investment risks for bonds are interest rate fluctuations and credit risk. The less apparent risk for bonds is the long-term loss of purchasing power due to inflation.

Stocks do not provide for a specific rate of return over a specific period nor for a return of investment principal. Theoretically, stocks have unlimited potential for capital appreciation, but they also have a bottom; they can go to zero and become worthless. The obvious risk for stocks is short-term volatility or price fluctuation. Last and most important, stocks are the only investment vehicles that offer the potential for real total return: capital gains dividends dividend growth.

Total Return

No one has tomorrow's newspaper, so the future is uncertain. What we do have is historical data, which may or may not be applicable to today's economic environment. We know, however, that the markets are a discounting mechanism that takes both past history and current conditions into consideration in an attempt to discern the future.

Although the review of various rolling holding periods indicates that, in the overwhelming majority of instances, stocks significantly outperform bonds on a nominal and after-inflation basis, stocks can and have suffered significant losses on a calendar-year basis.

In short, there is no free lunch. When you put your money to work in the financial markets, it will be exposed to risk. However, risk, when properly understood, can be used to your advantage. The difference between success and failure in the stock market ultimately comes down to three things: knowledge, strategy, and tactics.

When you understand the differences between stocks and bonds, the advantages and disadvantages, the risks and rewards, that is knowledge. With knowledge you can devise a plan of attack, which is a strategy. Confident in your knowledge and with a proven strategy at the ready, you are prepared to initiate the procedures to implement your strategy. Those are tactics.

In the next chapter I detail the dividend-value strategy that we advocate in Investment Quality Trends and utilize at Private Client.

The Dividend-Value Strategy

Any serious student of the stock market and investment history is undoubtedly aware of the vast collection of colorful characters that have achieved either fame, infamy, or both for their spectacular successes and/or even more spectacular failures. Many of these stories are true; an equal number, perhaps more, are myths.

Whether these stories are true is unimportant, what these characters represent is: winning and losing. Everybody loves a winner and more often than not we in the United

States turn them into heroes. When it comes to investing in the stock market, however, many investors can more readily identify with the losers than the winners, which is unfortunate.

Losing money hurts more than just the pocket book; it vexes the soul. When you take a loss in the stock market, it is not uncommon to feel a variety of emotions: anger, guilt, perhaps humiliation. The fact is that, if you invest long enough, you are going to take your share of losses; nobody gets a free pass.

No matter your level of intelligence, success in the stock market can be elusive and transitory. Over the course of my career I have met many people who were flat out brilliant in their field of endeavor, yet who were completely hapless when it came to in- vesting in the stock market. In many cases, these brilliant people, who in the rest of their life have experienced nothing but success, have chosen to throw in the towel and just give up, which was unfortunate and entirely unnecessary.

What few investors understand is that the stock market is the grandest of competitions, the game of all games, played out on a global scale. As anyone who has evercompeted on any level knows, every game has its rules! In the stock market, as in any other competitive situation, the best players—the winners—are those who have knowledge and a strategy. Winning, not surprisingly, is much easier with the right strategy. Obviously there are some major differences between investing in the stock market and a simple pastime. For one, the stakes are higher—the potential loss of hard- won earnings, savings, and security both now and in the future.

But for the winner, the rewards are also higher. Beyond the gain in wealth, few things are more satisfying than the thrill of the hunt, the joy of discovery, and the lasting satisfaction of a victory that is heightened because of the importance of this endeavor. And win¬ning is much easier with the right strategy.

The Two Paths of Stock Return

Most investors who buy stocks do so with the hope of realizing a good rate of return. Hope, however, is not a strategy. For the investor who chooses the stock market as the avenue to grow their wealth, it is important to understand the elements that comprise the return on investment in stocks. More often than not, the most tangible element of return, the dividend, goes underappreciated.

All stock investors want the price of their stocks to increase, but stock prices don't rise because of simple desire; they need a catalyst, a reason for investors to buy and push the price higher. The underlying premise of the dividend-value strategy is that the dividend yield is the major driver for the price of a stock. Think about it: All things being equal, when is a stock most attractive to investors? When its dividend yield is high. An attractive dividend and high-yield is all but impossible for savvy investors to ignore. As the lure of securing a high yield attracts investors, the price of the stock begins to move higher. As price and yield have an inverse relationship, climbing stock prices result in declining yields. When the yield declines to a level where it is no longer enticing, investor interest, and therefore buying, disappears.

Without investor demand, the price of the stock will begin to decline until it reaches a price point where the yield is again sufficient to attract new buying interest.

When compared to the analytical systems that focus on price patterns, a company's products and services, price/earnings to growth (PEG) ratios, earnings yield, or a host of other measures, the elegant simplicity of focusing on the dividend yield emerges. That is, knowing that a stock is attractive when the dividend yield is high and unattractive when it is low provides the investor an objective measure of whether a stock's price is high, low, or somewhere in between. Because the relationship between price and yield is the centerpiece of the dividend-value strategy, it makes sense to flesh out the related concepts in detail.

There are two components that comprise the return on a stock market investment. Not surprisingly, the one most investors focus on is capital or price appreciation; everyone wants to sell a stock for a profit. The other component is the dividend, which represents an immediate return on investment. When combined into one measure, the two components become what is known as the total return. I think it is fairly safe to say that every time an investor buys a share of stock he does so with the absolute certainty that he will sell it later at a profit. Over time, after the inevitable loss or losses, the illusion of certainty is replaced with the wisdom that is gained only through experience; namely, in the stock market, nothing is certain. What isn't illusory, though, is the dividend. Once received the dividend is yours to keep, a tangible return on investment that the market can't snatch away from you as it can a paper profit.

Dividend Yield

Company Price Dividend Dividend Yield

Trinity Corp. $44 $1.60 3.63%

Keegan, Inc. $76 $1.80 2.36%

Jillian, Ltd. $18 $1.28 7.11%

Evan Industries $69 $2.72 3.94%

Christian & Co. $25 $1.64 6.56%

Now that you understand what a dividend is and how to calculate the return in terms of yield, let's look closer at the relationship between price, yield, and value. Let's take two stocks, one priced at $10 a share that pays a $.50 dividend and one priced at $20 that pays a $1 dividend.

Beyond the fact that $20 is twice that of $10 and $1 is twice that of $.50, they have equal value in terms of dividend yield; both pay 5.0 percent dividends. Because stock prices and dividends rarely fall into such easy-to-calculate round numbers as in the previous example, let's look at some more examples of how the dividend yield is calculated. Remember, yield is calculated on the price paid for the stock, so unless there is a change in the dividend, the yield on purchase remains constant no matter what the stock's current price is. The company names in this example are fictitious.

Whether dividends or capital appreciation is your favored comoponent of return, you still need a means by which to define and identify the value for any stock under investment consideration.

Measures of Value

Traditionally there are three fundamental measurements of value: price-to-earnings ratio (P/E), price-to-book ratio (PB), and dividend yield. What is immediately apparent with the two ratios is that they are centered on price. Price, without substantive context, is meaningless. Of the three measures, the dividend yield is the only one related to an actual return on investment the dividend payment. So beyond the value of the income to the investor, dividends provide tangible evidence that the company is actually making money, which is something that an earnings statement or book values cannot prove.

Quality of Earnings

Earnings are the lifeblood of every company and the sole reason the company exists—to generate a profit. With earnings, however, what is real and what is reported can be two entirely different things. That is, a corporate earnings statement can be a labyrinth to navigate through, with its seemingly endless collection of foot- notes, exceptions, and variables. In simple terms, earnings can be sliced and diced to the point where they are often unintelligible. Why is this? To be fair, a company's earnings can be impacted by myriad events ranging from the simple to very complex. A change in company leadership, for example, can lead to asset sales or a string of acquisitions. All these things must be duly noted; however, a recurring pattern of revisions and restatements might be indicative of less than forthright reporting. That earnings can be manip¬ulated is not in question; it happens frequently to varying degrees for varying reasons. To some this may appear cynical, but when you get down to the bottom line, earnings are often what a financial officer says they are.

Rising Dividends Boost Share Price

With the preceding text as a frame of reference, we see why dividend-yield trends are a more predictive indicator for stock price appreciation/depreciation. When a dividend is increased, the price of a stock (which generally represents current value) typically rises to reflect the increased value of the investment. Conversely, when a dividend is lowered, the stock price typically declines to reflect reduced investment value and expectations for further reductions in earnings, not to mention the loss of anticipated income to the investor. The only variable in this equation is the amount of time for the market to realize the increase/decrease in value and adjust the price accordingly.

Why Dividends Are So Important

"The proof is in the pudding boy,"was one of my grandfather's many folksy colloquialisms to make a point or teach a lesson. When applied to dividends, it underscores the point that they are tangible proof of a return on investment. When a company has a long¬term track record for consistent and rising dividend payments, there is simply no better indicator about the state of the company's financial health. Dividends are real money; the check either clears or it doesn't. Dividends prove the company is making money; you can't pay what you don't have. So instead of trying to determine profitability by studying a company's earnings, study its dividend history.

At the end of the day dividends are the surest confirmation of a company's profitability, since dividends can arise only from the reality of earnings.

Now let's take this a step further. If you stop and think about it, there is really only one reason a company's management and board of directors votes for a dividend increase—higher earnings or the reasonable expectation for higher earnings. Once again, the only variable is the amount of time it takes for the market to realize the increased value to the stock because of the dividend increase to push the price higher. This is where the virtue of patience is paramount.

Even if an investor doesn't require immediate income from his stocks, he can still appreciate that dividends provide a floor of safety under the price of a stock. From experience, we know that savvy market observers pay close attention to dividend yield, and when the price of a stock falls to a level that creates an attractive return, investment capital will flow into the stock and halt the decline. A stock that pays no dividend has no such downside protection for its price.

Total Return Revisited

it is central to the dividend-value strategy and the underlying justification for investing in the stock market. The primary advantage of a stock investment is the potential for total return:

Dividend yield^capital gains1/4total return

From the Dividend-Yield Theory comes another factor to add to that equation: dividend growth.

Dividend yield dividend growth^capital gains 1/4real total return The idea of real total return is, has been, and always will be the underlying reason why investors are willing to risk their capital in common stocks. It has been the fundamental attraction of stock market investments since they began.

Although the bond market can offer a fixed return and, depending on the trend in interest rates, some potential for capital gains, the growth of dividend income is only available in the stock market. As detailed earlier, dividend growth is the catalyst for and most accurate predicator of rising stock prices.

Over the course of the past 44 years there are untold examples of stocks that realized rates of real total return that would have been virtually impossible to obtain in any other investment vehicle with a commensurate degree of risk. These stocks had been held for several years, during which time there were consistent dividend increases, which precipitated consistent price increases. Here's an example to illustrate the point.

One of the world's most widely recognized brand names is that of McDonald's (MCD), which virtually created the quick-service restaurant industry and today operates and franchises about 32,000 restau¬rants in 118 countries.

Despite its history and status as the American icon company, McDonald's struggled during the late 1990s and early 2000s. Derided in some analytical corners as a relic of the past and a dying industry, McDonald's in many ways epitomized the shift in consumer attitudes away from the old-school brick-and mortar model to the new school of hip-slick-and-cool, as represented by Starbucks.

In 2003, McDonald's management decided it would not go quietly into the night and initiated a corporate strategy to put the luster back into the Golden Arches. Part of the strategy was a commitment to shareholders to increase the value of their investment through a combination of share buybacks and dividend increases; were they ever serious! In 2002 McDonald's (MCD) dividend was $0.06 per quarter or $0.24 per year. By the end of 2003 the dividend had been increased by 60 percent to $0.10 a quarter or $0.40 per year. The dividend has been consistently raised each year since, and through August 2009, the dividend was $.50 per quarter or $2.00 per year.

The first incremental dividend increase in 2003 put MCD into our undervalued area and on our radar screen. Our initial purchases were made at $15 per share and again at $19 per share. At the time of this writing, the stock is trading at $57, just shy of a 300 percent capital gain. More importantly, though, our initial dividend has increased by almost 1,000 percent and our yield on purchase is approximately 10 percent. Some readers are undoubtedly wondering why we haven't sold this stock to harvest the gains. As will be explained more thoroughly in later chapters, MCD still represents good historic value due to the frequency and size of dividend increases. Figure 3.1 shows a graphic display of this fundamental value in the accompanying chart. As you can see, the stock still has considerable upside potential.

With the potential for real total returns, such as those illustrated by the example of McDonald's, you begin to see how a stock that is held long enough for the concept to work can outpace the twin evils of taxes and inflation.

To be fair, we cannot be sure that dividends will rise in each and every year. We cannot be sure when and to what extent stock prices will rise. Indeed, since October 2007 the markets have been unde going the corrective process known as a bear market. However, if stocks are purchased at historically undervalued price levels, and if those stocks have a long, uninterrupted history of dividend payments and of frequent dividend increases, then over a period of years the real total return on that investment is likely to outperform the total return on any other kind of investment.

Quality Tells

Although the dividend-value strategy can be implemented with any company paying dividends long enough to establish a pattern, the chances for success are greater with blue-chip stocks. Forty-four years of market research show that the dividend-value strategy, when implemented through high-quality stocks with long track records for consistent dividend increases, provides a powerful tool for building wealth. In the end, it is the building of wealth, both capital and income to meet the present and future cash needs of the investor, that is most important.

Its practical application through the dividend-value strategy in generic terms. The simple premise is that a decision to buy or sell a stock at a certain price is tied to the underlying value of its dividends as expressed by the dividend yield.

The Holy Grail for all stock investors is to buy low and sell high. Unfortunately, for most investors, high and low are typically references for price. As stated previously, though, price without substantive context is meaningless. In 2003 McDonald's was undervalued at $15, but also at $19,because its dividend yield represented historically good value. The same was true in 2004 at $40 and again in 2009 at $57. So without a way to measure value, high and low are nothing but nebulous concepts.

From our perspective, this is fairly simple stuff; the theory and strategy are pretty basic to investing. Maybe it's too basic, because the simplicity often confuses investors who seem determined to find a more complicated method for growth of capital and income and, ultimately, financial security. For over 44 years though, when the concept is applied to high-quality dividend trends, it can help the investor to:

- Minimize downside risk in the stock market
- Maximize upside potential for capital gains
- Maximize growth of dividend income, which allows investors to keep pace with inflation

The Natural Order

The Tax Reform Act of 2003 dramatically lowered the rate of federal income tax levied against dividends received from qualifying companies. For those who believe dividends are a waste of corporate capital, the commonly heard refrain since passage of the Act is "watch what happens to dividend-paying stocks when Congress returns the tax rate to pre-Act levels."

The fact of the matter is that Congress is continually tinkering with the tax code. Depending on the administration and your philosophical side of the aisle, these adjustments can be perceived as positive, negative, or neutral. However, some fail to remember that the markets are dynamic, constantly adjusting to economic fluctuation, legislation, taxation, and innovation; in short, the markets adjust.

Detractors also forget that investors have flocked to dividends since investment records have been kept, so the philosophy that the dividend yield of a quality company can reveal volumes about a stock's future performance is not dependent on a certain tax environment or a particular market cycle. It is a basic principle, one that serves as a consistent guide through even the most frustrating market phases.

"The underlying principles of sound investment should not alter from decade to decade," writes Benjamin Graham in his classic work,The Intelligent Investor,"but the application of these principles must be adapted to significant changes in the financial mechanisms and climate."

Dividends Still Don't Lie

A lot of water has passed beneath the bridge since Geraldine Weiss first wrote Dividends Don't Liein 1988. Investment theories have come and gone, various trading techniques and alternative investment vehicles have enjoyed a brief moment in the investment sun only to be abandoned when proven imperfect or ineffective, and investors have flocked to and fled from myriad fads, phenomena, and false hope. Through it all, one thing has remained constant—the dividend. Dividends are still the most reliable component of investment return because dividends are still real money. Balance sheets and earnings statements can weave visions of grandeur but they don't put money in your pocket. When a company pays a dividend, it can't be revised or restated. Once a dividend leaves the company bank, it is irretrievable. No number of adjustments, schemes, or tricks can be used to fudge a dividend payment; it's either paid or it isn't. In short, dividends tell a truth that no company report can.

In the wake of the Enron and World-Com scandals at the start of the decade and the more recent meltdowns in the banking and credit industries, corporate management and boards of directors are under greater scrutiny than in any previous period in financial market history. As such, ever-greater care and deliberation is being given to the declaration and payment of dividends.

Even without this heightened scrutiny, the management and directors of quality corporations know far better than anyone else the financial condition of their company and the likely direction that future earnings will take. Given the apparent ramifications of pending legislation alongside those existing in Sarbanes-Oxley, competent, well-managed blue chip companies with long track records of excellence and performance are not going to pay or increase a dividend unless the payout is fiscally justified and sound. For these reasons, a trend of consistently rising dividends is more indicative of a company's health and well being than any other measure. For the investor seeking a reliable return on investment from a predictable stream of dividends, there is an added bonus: A trend of rising dividends is also a reliable predictor for future capital growth.

At this juncture, you should have a solid grasp on the concepts that dividends and dividend yields are a component of return, a measure of value, and a predictor of growth. Going forward we explain how to apply these concepts to the process of building a portfolio, managing the portfolio through various market cycles, and anticipating future share price and market directions.

CHAPTER 2

Finding Undervalued and Overvalued Stocks

One need not be a market wizard to understand that for every stock there are optimum times to buy and sell. For the investor whose primary objective is to maximize capital gains and to capture as much dividend income and growth possible, it is imperative to establish the repetitive areas of undervalue and overvalue.

Although capital gains can be achieved in stocks that are not purchased at undervalued levels, the potential for upside is reduced and the downside risks are increased. In a rising market, an investor may get away with this practice for a time, but one too many trips to that well and investment capital can disappear in a hurry. That is to say, there is a higher probability for consistent growth of capital and income when the investor maintains a buying and selling discipline based on the understanding of values.

In our experience, the most reliable way to identify stocks that offer good values is to limit investment considerations to only the highest-quality stocks and then establish the repetitive patterns of dividend yield, which reveals the areas of undervalue and overvalue. For some, this process, which you know now as the dividend-value strategy, can be viewed as overly mechanical or perhaps even rigid, but there is a method to the madness. Even seasoned investors can be seduced by the energy and momentum of a fast-moving market and be tempted to follow the crowd.

Those are the instances when most investors make mistakes that can inflict long-lasting damage to a portfolio. With the calm objec- tivity that comes from an adherence to quality and value, however, investors can avoid the pitfalls that derail others from reaching their ultimate objective, building a pool of wealth from which to secure current and future cash needs.

Finding and buying a stock that is undervalued requires patience and fortitude. For the investor who can master these virtues, the rewards are well worth the time and effort. In this chapter, we focus on how to

identify the four categories of value: Undervalued, the Rising Trend, Overvalued, and the Declining Trend. Although it is important to recognize and understand the rising and declining trends, the majority of this chapter is directed toward undervalue and overvalue. In later chapters, we discuss how to incorporate our understanding of these four categories of value into the dividend value portfolio.

A Sophisticated Approach

As mentioned in previous chapters, most stock market analysis is conducted through either fundamental or technical analysis. The dividend-value strategy is a marriage between the two disciplines. Although the process of identifying historic parameters of value by charting the highs and lows of dividend yield is clearly technical, our insistence that explorations for value be limited to only those stocks worthy of Select Blue Chip status is rooted in the most basic of fundamentals, the dividend, which represents a spendable return on investment capital.

Each stock has its own profile of undervalue and overvalue dividend yield, which means each stock must be studied individually. Any investor can establish the dividend-yield profile of any stock that has paid a dividend over sufficient time to establish a pattern. To identify these patterns you must first compute the dividend yield over a decade or longer (15 to 25 years is optimum) and then chart the channels on a grid.

At Investment Quality Trends, we have a fairly sophisticated algorithm that identifies the low- price/high-yield areas and the high- price/low-yield areas. In the "old days" this process required mastery of a slide rule; for a period we rented time on the old Computer Data computers that were programmed by punch cards. Geraldine has often said that the greatest invention of all time was the hand-held calculator, which dramatically shortened the process. Today, we have the luxury of a computer workstation.

As with most stock charts, the price is found on the left (vertical) axis, and time is displayed along the bottom (horizontal) axis. The first step is to identify all the high-price extremes and the low-price extremes. In this example, we would note the highs in 1999, 2002, and 2007. For the lows we would note 2000 and 2008. The second step is to find the high price for each high-price year and the low price for each low-price year. These prices would be $49.25, $53.52, and $105.02 for the years 1999, 2002, and2007, respectively. The data points for the low price areas in this example are $23 in 2000 and $50.71 in 2008. The third step is to find the dividend paid for each year of data points and then to calculate the dividend yield for each point. These would be 1.42 percent, 1.53 percent, and 1.41 percent for the highs and 3.21 percent and 3.47 percent for the lows.

Beginning with the high-price data points we add the three dividend yields together and then divide by three,finding an average of 1.45 percent.

Unfortunately, due to space limitations in presenting the charts, what you don't see in this example is that this stock in 1987 and 1992 recorded low yields of 1.60 percent. Since there is a divergence between 1.45 percent and 1.60 percent, we would like to find a confirmation of the low yields recorded in 1987 and 1992. By adding a fourth yield from the 2005 high price, which is 1.89 percent, then dividing by four, we find an average of 1.56 percent, which we will round up to 1.60 percent and, therefore, confirm that the 1.60 percent dividend yield is the repetitive low.

Now, turning to the low-price/high-yield data points, we note that there are three minor lows (2001, 2003, and 2005) between the major lows in 2000 and 2008. When we calculate the dividend yields for these periods we find a major divergence. Hence, we discard these three and focus on the two extremes in 2000 and 2008. By adding these two yields together and then dividing by 2 we find an average of 3.34 percent, which we will round down to 3.30 percent. Once again, by looking back to 1987, 1988/1989, and to 1990, we find additional instances where the 3.30 percent dividend yield has marked a halt in declining prices and the stock reversed course, confirming that this is the high- yield undervalue area for this stock.

Undervalued Stocks

Using the simplest definition, undervalue is a relatively high dividend yield that in the past has coincided with the bottom of a major price decline. The term can apply to an individual stock, a group of stocks, or the overall market. When these repetitive areas of high- dividend yield are plotted on a stock chart, it becomes visually apparent that the stock has a tendency toward halting and reversing a decline in the same relative area of dividend yield each cycle. By averaging these relative areas of high yield, a boundary for the bottom can be established.

To further illustrate this point, let's consider the example of a company we will call Widgets "R" Us. In 1999, the stock recorded a 2.5 percent yield, which represented the top price for that cycle. In 2003, 2005, and 2007, the stock recorded low yields of 2.5 percent, 2.3 percent, and 2.7 percent, respectively. In 2002 a decline in the stock was halted and reversed at a 5.0 percent dividend yield, in 2004 at a 4.8 percent yield, and again in 2004 at a 5.2 percent dividend yield.

When we average these respective areas of high and low yield, it suggests that Widgets "R" Us has a tendency to halt and reverse a declining trend in the 5.0 percent dividend-yield area and a rising trend at the 2.5 percent dividend-yield area. Note that dividend yield is calculated from both price and dividend; as such the price of the stock at each of those turning points can vary depending on the dollar amount of the dividend. The Stanley Works (SWK) offers good historic value when the dividend yield is at 5.0 percent. The stock reaches its historic level of overvalue when the price rises and the dividend yield declines to 2.0 percent.

In October of 2000, The Stanley Works (SWK) declined to a price of $18.80. Based on the annual dividend of $0.94, the dividend yield was 5.0 percent and the stock was historically undervalued, which is displayed in the following equation:

Dividend Price Yield

$O:94=$I8:8OI/45:O percent

A 5.0 percent dividend yield also identified historic good value in 2003, 2008, and 2009.

If there were one high yield that identified an undervalued price for every stock, it would make life ever so much simpler. Unfortunately, that just isn't the case. Because each stock has a unique profile of value, based on its repetitive extremes of high and low dividend yield, undervalue is not simply a very low price; rather, it represents a relatively high yield in relation to a currently low price. This is what makes an undervalued stock a bargain—high-quality at good value at a low price.

To take full advantage of the dividend-yield strategy, you will have to put in some work, which at the very least means keeping track of the undervalue and overvalue boundaries on the stocks under investment consideration. Once a purchase is made, you must continue to monitor the stock as it winds its way through its cycle. When dividends are increased, the yields at undervalue and overvalue must be recalculated to avoid selling your position too soon or to add to the position if a short-lived dip in price provides another undervalued opportunity.

As we did with The Stanley Works (SWK) example, we have identified the Profiles of Value for 272 additional Select Blue Chips. Based on the current dividend yield, each of these stocks are categorized as Undervalued, in Rising Trends, Overvalued, or in Declining Trends. Beyond the respective category of value, the data tables display current prices, dividends, yields, trailing 12- month earnings, book values, and other fundamental information.

Are the Numbers Chiseled in Stone?

An undervalued stock should never be purchased before considering other factors, particularly when the market is at or close to the top of its cycle. Upon further investigation, you may discover serious fundamental problems within the company that have forced the price to drop to undervalued levels. A high level of debt or an excessively high payout ratio may indicate the dividend is in danger. In general, however, if the stock is a blue chip and its dividend is well protected by earnings, a purchase at undervalued levels is definitely worthy of consideration.

When a high-quality stock such as SWK has declined to its under- valued area, the likelihood for a deeper decline in price is greatly reduced, but is by no means eliminated.

Although the repetitive points of undervalue and overvalue are established over long periods of time, the prices designating undervalue and overvalue levels are not chiseled in stone.

Remember, the markets are a reflection of the thoughts, opinions, and emotions of millions of investors, who can display a wide range of behaviors at any given moment. Yes, Virginia, the markets are sometimes even irrational. As such, investors can drive prices above or below undervalue and overvalue areas by a few points or even to ridiculous extremes.

Depending on how investors react to news and information, no power on earth can limit price movements between specific boundaries. If nothing else has been learned over the course of the present bear market, when sufficiently exercised, investors have the ability to move prices beyond logical norms and to speculative extremes.

As a case in point, observe the chart of UTX in Figure 7.4. Note that UTX offers good historic value when the dividend-yield is 2.2 percent and reaches its historic level of overvalue when the price rises and the yield declines to 1.2 percent. When the market re-opened after the September 11, 2001 attacks, UTX declined along with broad market to just above $20 per share.

Based on the then-current dividend of $0.45, the dividend yield reached 2.2 percent and the stock offered good historic value. The following bar, which represents the month of October, illustrates that investors were motivated sufficiently to accumulate UTX, and the price rose until April, 2002 to within 10 percent of its historic level of overvalue. At this juncture, the broad market turned down to test the September 2001 lows, and UTX followed suit until October 2002, within 10 percent of the undervalue yield of 2.2 percent. Almost on cue, the stock reversed to the upside and entered a rising trend, which was aborted in February 2003 when the markets tested the October 2002 lows.

In March 2003, the stock reached the undervalue yield of 2.2 percent and again reversed to the upside, quickly entering into a rising trend, which it sustained until October 2007, when the wheels began to fall off in the broad market. In July 2008, United Technologies Corporation had declined to the 2.2 percent under- value yield and reversed course in line with its well-established pattern. In September 2008, the broad market began what is referred to as a waterfall, and it declined until the halt and reversal on March 9, 2009.

If you remember, it was in September 2008, when Lehmann Brothers filed for bankruptcy and the banking, credit, and investment markets were turned upside down. As is illustrated on this chart, investors reacted to this event and those that quickly followed suit in an extremely negative fashion, driving UTX well beyond its historically repetitive undervalue yield of 2.2 percent. The fact that UTX, a member of the DJIA with an A+ quality ranking, had an uninterrupted string of earnings and dividend increases for the previous 10 years and a much longer history of superior performance prior to those 10 years was completely ignored by investors in an emotion-driven panic. At the time of this writing in mid-September 2009, UTX is trading at just shy of $63 per share and appears on track to resume its long-established Profile of Value.

In the vast majority of instances, overvalue and undervalue designations come within ten percent of the high or low in a major price move. As such, the Dividend-Yield Theory considers prices to be undervalued or overvalued when they are within the 10 percent range of their historic levels of high or low dividend yield.

The Market of Stocks

As mentioned previously, there is the stock market and there is the market of stocks. As such, good values can be found at virtually any phase of the stock market cycle. However, more undervalued stocks can be found at the end of a bear market or during a major correction in a bull market. Because the selection of undervalued stocks is likely to be large, it is a time that investors have an exceptional opportunity to diversify their holdings.

By example, in the mid-March 2009 issue of Investment Quality Trends,177 or 65 percent of our 273 Select Blue Chips represented historic good values and were in the Undervalued category. An extraordinary number, too many to list, were trading at or below book values. Also, extraordinary, as was illustrated in the UTX example, were the number of stocks investors had driven beyond long-established extremes of high dividend yield.

Although the Dividend-Yield Theory has accurately defined the repetitive levels of undervalue time and again over four decades, it cannot determine precisely when a stock purchased at undervalue will begin to rise in price. Nonetheless, it is clear that these stocks are bargains, and that high-quality stocks that have consistently proved their worth over the years will eventually garner investor attention.

As all experienced investors know, timing is almost impossible to nail down on a consistent basis. Even so, when the timing of an acquisition is not exactly in synch with that of the broad market trend, undervalued stocks have a propensity for maintaining their value and price, which can even be seen in a bear market. As my partner Mike frequently says, "With undervalued stocks it is a when and not an if." If there is one thing knowledgeable investors cannot ignore for very long, it is a high-quality company that offers exceptional, historic value. Although all economic and business cycles eventually come to an end and the markets will respond with a period of contraction, the conditions that initiated the decline will improve, and animal spirits will gravitate toward undervalued stocks to realize excellent long-term capital gains.

The Overvalued Phase

Using the simplest definition, overvalue is a relatively low dividend- yield that in the past has coincided with the top of a major rising price trend. The term can apply to an individual stock, a group of stocks, or the overall market. When these repetitive areas of low- dividend yield are plotted on a stock chart, it becomes visually apparent that the stock has a tendency toward halting and reversing a rising trend in the same relative area of dividend-yield each cycle.

By averaging these relative areas of low-yield, a boundary for the top can be established.

The process for identifying the historically repetitive areas of overvalue is identical to that for the historically repetitive areas of undervalue detailed earlier in this chapter. For a refresher, refer back to Figure 7.1 and the accompanying text.

For an example of overvalue, refer back to the undervalued stocks section and review the examples for the fictitious Widgets "R" Us and the real-world example of The Stanley Works (SWK). The mechanics for identifying Undervalue and overvalue are the same; the only difference is with overvalue you are looking for tops rather than bottoms.

When a stock approaches the undervalue area it is a signal to investors that historic good value is in the offing. Conversely, when a stock approaches the overvalue area, it is a signal to investors that much of the historic value has been realized over the course of the rising trend. This is not to say that that an overvalued stock cannot continue to rise; our charts are replete with dozens of examples that prove otherwise. What is fundamental to the overvalue area, however, is any further upside potential is far outweighed by the downside risk. The only caveat to this is if an overvalued company increases its dividend, the price at overvalue will also rise, creating further upside potential for the continuation of the rising trend.

Any experienced investor with an ounce of self-honesty will admit to have engaged in speculative roulette at some point in his invest- ment experience; anyone who has felt the energy and excitement of a rampaging stock or market knows exactly what I am referring to. Once euphoria sets in, however, it is much like unwanted company; hard to get rid of. Although everyone enjoys feeling on top of the world, for investors it can present a major problem because invest- ment euphoria often masks the fact that the top of a cycle has been reached. For the investor with eyes to see, the overvalued area is the time to ring the bell and plant theflag, meaning that it's time to harvest well-deserved profits.

The overvalue area also tends to coincide with the time that less sophisticated investors succumb to the allure of the large sums of money being made all around them, which all too often leads them to buy at the top. This phenomenon is most prevalent in the hot stock of the times, which perpetuates even more buying, which pushes stock prices beyond all measures of fundamental value. At some point, though, comes the inevitable correction; trees cannot grow to the sky.

When the broad market is overvalued, the risk level for all stocks is ratcheted higher. However, investment decisions should still be based on the specific values for individual stocks. Remember, each stock has its own distinctive level of overvalue. So, even when a bull market is in its latter stages, not all stocks are overvalued. For the ones that are overvalued, not all stocks are overvalued to the same extent.

For these reasons, it is important to plot each stock's dividend yield on a chart and make note of the yield area where the stock historically reverses course. In so doing, it is possible to identify the dividend yield at which it is overvalued. When a stock's price is pushed to the upper channel line on the dividend-yield charts shown in this book, the yield is reaching a level at which the investor is overpaying for the dividend to be received. This is the textbook portrait for the historically repetitive area of overvalue. See Figure 7.5 for a list of Overvalued stocks as of mid-September 2009.

No One Gets Bonus Points for Being a Hero

Of my grandfather's many lessons, the one most constantly re- inforced was "the gain is made on the buy, son." Although most of my grandfather's folksy quips of wisdom are immediately under- stood, whenever I share this one it almost always is met with a blank stare of confusion. "How do you establish a gain on the buy? You don't know what you've made until you sell!"

In the accounting sense, this, of course, is correct. What my grandfather was teaching me though was a values-based mindset; when you buy right, the gains are almost assured. In IQ Trends speak we would say that when you focus on quality and value there is a higher probability that gains will follow. In either case, the point should be easy to understand: The maximum potential for capital appreciation and the highest dividend yields are secured when a stock is purchased at historically good value.

So what is buying right? According to the Dividend- Yield Theory, stocks trade between two channels of dividend-yield extremes: An area of low price/high yield (undervalue), and an area of high price/ low yield (overvalue). Therefore, purchases should be limited to shares that offer historically repetitive high dividend yields and low prices (undervalue), which offers the maximum upside potential and minimum downside risk. That is buying right.

The corollary to buying right is obviously selling right. When a stock or a market reaches its overvalue phase, investors should be planning their exit rather than searching for new acquisitions. Let's be clear about one thing—the market isn't going anywhere. If you've gone to the trouble of sifting through dozens of stocks to find the few that are worthy of your investment capital, bought right, and sat patiently through the rising trend until the historic level of overvalue is reached, you've done your job; now collect your rewards. That is selling right.

Value can always be found in the stock market. As Geraldine has told me many times, "stocks are like streetcars, another will come along soon." It takes courage to purchase a stock at undervalue, it takes wisdom to sell it at overvalue.

The Rising Trend

Once a stock has moved up 10 percent or more off of its undervalued base, it has entered into a rising trend. As undervalue represents the buying area and overvalue represents the selling area, the rising trend can generally be characterized as the hold area. From the Investment Quality Trends perspective, a stock remains in a rising trend until it comes within 10 percent of its historically repetitive area of overvalue or falls back to within 10 percent of its undervalued area.

As any veteran market observer knows, stocks rarely move in a straight line from point A to point B. In fact, a stock may enter into a rising trend only to fall back to the undervalue area on a broad market decline. On the other hand, a stock can remain above its undervalue area in a rising trend for an extended period of time, moving sideways until the price breaks out and resumes its upward climb.

When making investment considerations, an investor should always look to stocks that are under valued first because they represent historically repetitive extremes of low price and high dividend yield. In some cases, however, when a stock is near its undervalued area yet technically in a Rising Trend, there may still be a viable opportunity to make a profitable purchase. Before making such a purchase decision though, there are two important things to take into consideration. The first is the primary trend of the broad market. Is it in a bull cycle or a bear cycle? In most cases it is best to avoid purchasing rising-trend stocks in a bear market because the overall wave of selling can engulf the stock, which will halt and reverse the upward trend. In this instance the stock can return to its undervalued area, which necessarily results in a loss to the investor.

Secondly, what is the upside potential to overvalue for the stock versus the downside risk back to undervalue for the stock? In this case, when the primary trend is up or in a bull cycle, stocks in a rising trend may still offer an attractive buying opportunity. The salient question at this point is how far into the rising trend the stock has traveled.

When the broad market is at undervalue or early in its rising trend and a stock is within 15 percent of its undervalued area, a purchase could still realize significant gains. This is particularly true if the stock has a long history of dividend increases. As referenced earlier, a dividend increase will lift the prices at undervalue and overvalue, which provides an additional layer of safety to the original investment. Also previously noted, dividend increases are a predictor for future price growth, not to mention the increased income, which can add momentum to the uptrend.

In October of 2002, a decline in EMR was halted within 10 percent of its undervalued yield of 4.0 percent, from which it entered into a rising trend. This advance was halted as the broad market moved lower in a test of the 2002 lows before reversing in March 2003 and resuming its upward move. Brief pullbacks in 2004 and 2005 offered additional buying opportunities as rising dividends moved the boundaries for undervalue and overvalue higher.

In 2006, EMR reached overvalue again and began the expected decline. However, the rising trend resumed as further dividend increases provided additional upside potential. In 2007, EMR breached the overvalue level on the strength of its dividend increases, and while it declined with the broad market in early 2008, investors pushed the stock into a rising trend one more time before the weight of the bear market broke its ascent and it declined to its undervalued area of 4.0 percent in 2009.

When the broad market stabilized and reversed course in March 2009, EMR followed suit. As of mid- September 2009, EMR has once again moved into a rising trend. When the broad market is in a rising trend, stocks that are in a rising trend can provide excellent short-term profit opportunities. A rising- trend stock in a rising-trend market has a greater chance to reach overvalue in a shorter period of time than an undervalued stock because it has a shorter distance to travel and it has the all- important force of market momentum at its back.

Value, Cycles, and the Dow Jones Averages

To narrow our considerations to only the highest quality blue chips we use the Criteria for Select Blue Chips. To identify historically repetitive areas of undervalue and overvalue of dividend yield we use the Dividend-Yield Theory. By combining the fundamental qualities of the Criteria with the technical attributes of the Dividend-Yield Theory we have the components of the dividend-value strategy.

In addition, to identifying the areas of undervalue and overvalue for individual stocks, the cyclical aspect of the Dividend-Yield Theory applies to the broad market, as measured by the Dow Jones Industrial Average (DJIA), in equal manner. By understanding the cyclic nature of value in the Dow, it allows the investor to further hone his buy, sell, and hold decisions. While many stocks will cycle through the phases of value contra to the primary trend of the broad market, it is no secret that it is easier to swim with the tide than against it. In the next chapter, I combine what has been written through this chapter into a roadmap for building and managing the dividend- value portfolio. Central to that discussion is the primary trend of the Dow, which phase of value is currently in force, and how this information should be included in your buy, sell, and hold considerations.

Because there are so many references to the DJIA throughout this book, there are undoubtedly some critics who will suggest that another index, such as the S&P 500 or perhaps the Dow Jones/ Wilshire 5000, would be more appropriate as a proxy for the overall market. While the S&P and Wilshire are important comparative measurements (the S&P 500 in particular, as it is the most widely recognized benchmark that most equity managers compare performance to), the DJIA has more of the blue chip quality characteristics that we are interested in and is still the most widely recognized of all market indexes.

As understanding the primary trend and current phase of value of the Dow is so important to the dividend- value investor, in Chapter 5 I illustrated the historically repetitive patterns of dividend yield that marked areas of undervalue and overvalue for the DJIA between 1926 and 1995. Also noted in Chapter 5, between 1995 and 2008 there was a divergence in this pattern, which requires an explanation. It is my belief that the DJIA is now in the process of reverting back to the historic pattern prior to 1995. If my assumption is correct, I feel it is incumbent to discuss what this portends for the remainder of the present bear market and how to prepare for the bull market that will eventually follow.

Before we dive into this section however, I want to provide a brief history of Charles Henry Dow, the genesis of the Dow Jones indexes, and Dow's contribution to value investing.

Charles H. Dow and the Dow Jones Averages

Charles Henry Dow was not an investment banker, a money manager, or a stockbroker. He was the son of a poor farmer who died when Charles was six years old.

Wanting more than the hard farming life that killed his father, he struck out at the age of 16 to become a newspaper man, although he had no formal education in journalism or even much formal education to speak of.

Be that as it may, Charles managed to find work as a reporter for several newspapers, including the Springfield Daily Republican and the Providence Journal. He left Providence and moved to New York, where he was employed by the Kiernan News Agency, a company that gathered and disseminated the financial news of the day. Also employed by Kiernan was a fellow by the name of Edward D. Jones, who Dow had known in the newspaper business in Providence. In 1882, Dow, Jones, and a third man named Charles Berg- stresser formed Dow Jones & Company. In 1884 Dow Jones published its first average of U.S. stocks in the Customer's Afternoon Letter,the forerunner to the Wall Street Journal. In 1886, Dow Jones published its first industrial average consisting of 12 companies that reflected a cross-section of industries.

The Index averaged the stocks of the following companies: American Cotton Oil, American Sugar, American Tobacco, Chicago Gas, Distilling & Cattle Feeding, Laclede Gas, National Lead, North American, Tennessee Coal, Iron and Railroad Company, U.S. Leather, U.S. Rubber, and General

Electric. Of these original 12, the lone survivor is General Electric.

According to a book titled The Dow Jones Averages that was published by Barron's in the early 1920s (another Dow Jones & Company publication), there are references to various stock aver- ages, comprised of as few as 12 stocks to as many as 60 stocks, that Dow experimented with as far back as 1872. Unfortunately, there is no record for what Dow's thinking was with these various averages, but one could conclude that he was searching for the appropriate mix of stocks that could reveal the primary trend of the market.

In any event, Dow must have found what he was looking for, and by 1897 there were dual Averages, the Industrial and the Railroad, the latter of which became the Transportation Average. In 1929, Dow Jones & Company introduced the Dow Jones Utility Average to track the utilities subset of the market.

Most of Dow's writings are not available, but 16 editorials were published in The ABC of Stock Speculation in 1903, a year after Dow's death, by S.A. Nelson. Although the conventional wisdom is that Dow was purely a technician (practitioner of technical analysis), which is obvious to the extent that Dow believed that his Averages, and the individual stocks from which they were comprised, were influenced by the cycles that coincided with bull and bear markets, he was also clearly cognizant of the importance of values. These discussions of values, along with the works of Benjamin Graham, greatly influenced my predecessor and mentor Geraldine Weiss and me. From these two academic fathers came the under-pinnings of the

Dividend-Yield Theory and Geraldine's original interpretation, which forms the approach outlined in this book and is promulgated by Investment Quality Trends.

If you refer back to the foreword to this book, Geraldine supplies the Dow quote that has graced the pages of our newsletter since inception and is one of our guiding principles: "The legendary Charles Dow has written,'To know values is to know the meaning of the market. And values, when applied to stocks, are determined in the end by the dividend yield.'"

Although the majority of Dow's legacy is attributed to the Wall Street Journal and the Dow Theory that bears his name, it is clear he understood the importance of values and that dividends are the primary indicator of value.

The Dividend-Yield Theory and the Dow Jones Industrial Average

Just as parameters of value can be established for individual stocks, so, too, can good buying and selling areas be established for the DJIA. From the early days of the stock market, the DJIA fluctuated between dividend-yield extremes of 6.0 percent and 3.0 percent, which represent undervalue and overvalue, respectively (see the charts in Figure 6.2). That profile of value guided the stock market through every bull and bear market from 1929 through 1995.

Prior to the current bear market, the worst bear market of modern times began in 1966 at an overvalue yield of 3.0 percent and was not completed until December, 1974 when the undervalue yield of 6.0 percent was reached.

From 1975 to 1982 the market fluctuated between dividend yield extremes of 5.0 percent and 6.0 percent until a new bull market was launched.

The bull market that began at undervalue in 1982 rose to over- value in 1992, remained there until 1995, and then a remarkable thing happened: For the first time in history the DJIA continued to ascend above its historically repetitive low yield and appeared to have formed a new profile of investment value. From the mid-1990s through September 2008, what formerly was the yield at overvalue (3.0 percent) became the new floor of undervalue and a dividend yield of 1.50 percent became the new selling area of overvalue.

In October 2008, however, the DJIA broke below 10.000 and eventually reached an intraday low price of 6440.08. Based on the composite dividend at that time, the dividend yield on the DJIA rose to 4.90 percent, a decisive violation of the undervalued dividend- yield floor of 3.0 percent.

A Long Blow-Off Top

When the long-term dividend-yield profile of the DJIA was violated in the early to mid-1990s, it came as a great shock. Intuitively, we knew something was amiss but we just couldn't put our finger on it. Because the new pattern persisted, we had to report it, but now that it appears there is a reversion to the mean, it begs an important question. What convinced the global body of investors to change their behavior after 60-plus years of predictability? In the rear view mirror in which all post mortems are conducted, the evidence points to the financial equivalent of the perfect storm.

By the mid-1990s, the ascension of the personal computer, operating systems that the average person could learn, along with associated software applications that increased productivity, launched a modern-day Industrial Revolution. With technology at their fingertips that was previously available to only the wealthiest of companies or individuals, the average person could now access the Internet and the Information Age was born.

News and financial information that once took weeks if not months to be disseminated and synthesized was now available in real time,to everybody. Simultaneous to this explosion of information technology and the industries that grew from it, an era offiscal responsibility (short-lived that it was) descended upon the halls of Congress. The promise of smaller government and balanced bud- gets lit afire under the bond market. Interest rates, which had already declined significantly since 1982, continued their down- ward trajectory.

The Federal Reserve Open Market Committee (the FOMC or more simply, the Fed), which at the time was led by Chairman Alan Greenspan, fell in love with this new-found productivity and for the most part remained accommodative. Oversight and regulation of the financial industry and markets by the Congress and other regulators was virtually nonexistent. Corporate and personal in- come taxes were generally low, and favorable tax treatment was afforded to capital gains. In retrospect, it is no wonder investors ignored the message of overvalue that a 3.0 percent dividend yield on the Dow represented.

Who cares about values and the meaning of dividends when the powers that be are aligned with the speculative stars? With the investment winds at their back and a tax code designed to ignore dividends and embrace capital gains, investors said to heck with values and plunged in with both feet; hence the tech and dot-com markets.

We should backtrack for a moment and revisit the environment from which the bull market that began in 1982 was launched. From 1966 through 1974 the market was decimated by a vicious bear cycle. By late 1974 the dividend yield on the Dow was 6.0 percent and our undervalued category was 80 percent of our Select Blue Chip universe. Between 1974 and 1982, the Dow fluctuated between dividend yields of 5 percent and 6 percent and our under- valued category fluctuated only slightly above and below the 80 percent level.

When the third and final leg down of the bear market began in 1973, the Undervalued category rose to dominance and remained there until the bull market began in 1982. As frustrated capital that had been pent up since the end of the bear in 1974 came rushing in, the Rising-Trends category eclipsed the Undervalued category as stock prices were pushed higher.

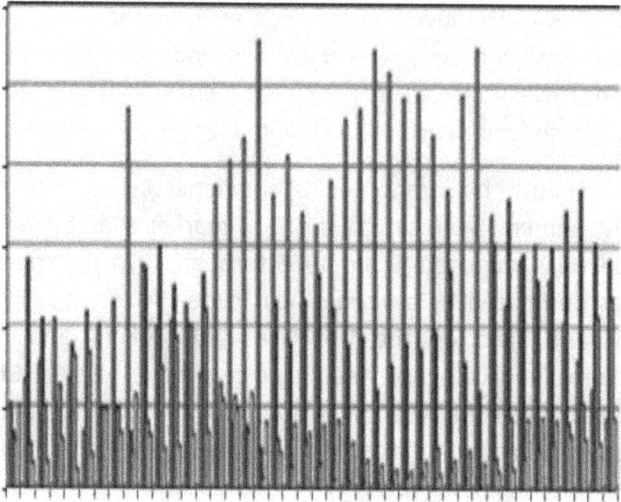

Now look at the bar graph in Figure 8.2 that illustrates the period from 1987 through July 2009 to see what happened to all of those historically good values.

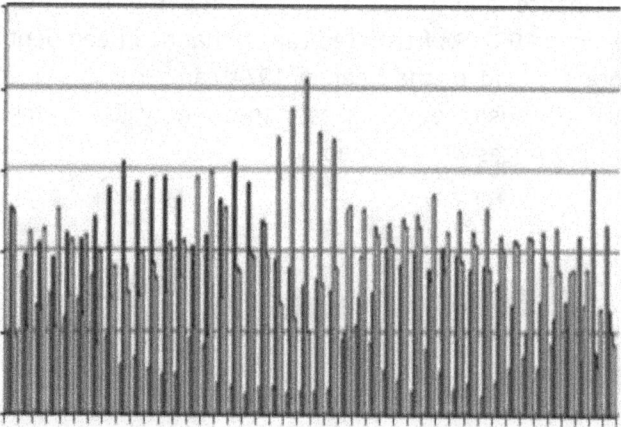

On the far left edge of Figure 8.2 is the reading from July 1987. Note that the Rising and Declining Trend categories are about even. The dividend yield on the Dow had breached the 3.0 percent overvalue yield at this point. The next set of bars represents the reading of January 1988. Here we can see that the crash on October 19, 1987 had moved the majority of stocks into declining trends and the dividend yield on the Dow had declined back to 4.0 percent. The readings from July 1988 and January 1989 depict similar levels of value to January 1988. By the January 1990 reading, the rising trends had reasserted their dominance and the dividend yield on the Dow had declined once again to the 3.0 percent overvalue area.

From mid-year 1994 through January 1995 the Declining-Trends category took center stage. There is really only one explanation for this: The majorities of Select Blue Chips had declined below over- value and were moving toward their respective areas of undervalue. You can almost sense that investors knew intuitively the market was overbought and needed to retrench.

Then the perfect storm, as described earlier, kicked into gear. From mid-year 1995 until mid-year 1997 the rising trends returned to the fore. At that point the dividend yield on the Dow was so low that well diggers would have had trouble finding it. From that point through early 2000, the Overvalue category reigned supreme as investors thoroughly trashed whatever could be trashed until the first leg down of the present bear market took hold.

In 2000, the luster and allure of quick profits in companies that were created on a cocktail napkin began to wear off. When earnings failed to materialize and the reality that, in many cases, these companies were simply speculations, the tech and dot-com illusion came to a screeching halt. By late 2000 and early 2001 it was clear the economy was in recession and the markets began to tumble in earnest. When America was attacked on September 11, 2001, the selling accelerated and the markets continued to decline through November 2002.

In response to recession and the market seizure as a result of 9/11, the Federal Reserve embarked on an unprecedented easing of Fed Fund rates. The only pool of capital readily available was tied up in home equity and the only way to unlock it was to drive interest rates down to Depression-era levels and to hold them there. In the name of market reform, the Tax Reform Act of 003 was passed and income tax rates on dividends and capital gains were lowered dramatically to stimulate investor interest. This Act, along with the tech and dot-com bust fresh in their minds, not to mention the Enron, World Com et al. scandals, encouraged investors to rediscover value stocks and dividends. As a result, high-quality dividend-paying blue chip stocks that had been virtually ignored during the decade of the 1990s were once again embraced, and shares appreciated dramatically.

Returning to the graph in Figure 8.2, we see that although investors had fallen in love with dividends again, in 2003 there was an obvious absence of anything that even remotely resembled historically good values. Also, when the first leg down bottomed in 2002 and retested in early 2003, the dividend yield on the Dowwas still below its historically repetitive area of overvalue dividend yield!

At the risk of being redundant, I need to drive this point home. Since 1966, when the Undervalue category represented 17 percent or less of our select blue-chip universe, it has been coincident with major market tops.

When the Undervalue category is between 70 percent and 80 percent of our universe, it has been coincident with major market bottoms. At the market top in 2000, our Under- value category was 12 percent of our universe. When the first leg down bottomed in late 2002 our Undervalue category still represented only 16 percent of our universe! So after dropping 5,000 points, the Dow was still dramatically overvalued! By mid-year 2005, our under-valued stocks had fallen further to only 4 percent of our universe. Now consider this: With the previous as a backdrop, the market continued to move higher for two more years. At this point the terms overvalue and irrational exuberance have no meaning; we are talking sheer insanity. Isn't it amazing what massive amounts of liquidity created by rock-bottom interest rates and the illusion of derivatives can create? Obviously some segment of investors had recognized that the massive leverage and speculation that had been compounding since the end of World War II had finally reached a tipping point. How can I write this? The majority of stocks in the Undervalue category were banks and other financials.

The Walls Come Tumbling Down

When housing prices had reached unsustainable levels and buyers were no longer able to flip at higher prices, it became clear that many of these buyers/borrowers were unable to meet and carry the debt service.

Subsequently the mortgage-backed securities that had been formed from these mortgages became suspect as the value of the underlying properties began to deteriorate. Banks, brokerage firms, and hedge firms that were heavily invested in these securities now had to mark-to-market, and with no reliable metric to value these properties and securities, the entire structure began to fall apart. For all intents and purposes what ensued was one giant margin call as everybody needed liquidity to shore up their balance sheets.

When one receives a margin call there are two options: sell positions or deposit more cash. Unable to sell their mortgage-backed securities, the banks, brokers, and hedge funds had to sell whatever they could—blue chip stocks, oil, gold, commodities, you name it. As the selling became a waterfall, the investing public began to hear about derivatives, synthetic securities with names like collateralized debt obligations (CDOs) and credit default swaps, which actually had been in use since the mid-1990s.

Institutions that at one time were believed to be too big to fail like Bear Sterns were absorbed, and Lehman Brothers declared bankruptcy. Merrill Lynch was acquired by Bank of America. Washington Mutual, which had raised its dividend over 40 consecutive quarters, was taken over by the FDIC and sold to JP Morgan Chase for next to nothing.

The End Game

My thought is the market pattern that is developing is similar to that of the bear market from 1966 through 1974. This is not to say I expect the bear market to last for eight years, but that I suspect the Dow will go through a similar sequence of three down legs inter-spersed by two highly profitable counter-trend rallies until the dividend yield on the Dow declines to between 5.0 percent and 6.0 percent, which should set the stage for a new bull market.

For a point of reference, let's look at the chart in Figure 8.3, which illustrates the pattern described earlier in the 1966-1974 bear market.

The bear market began in 1966 when the dividend- yield on the Dow declined to its historically repetitive area of overvalue at 3.0 percent. The first leg down was completed later that year and reversed course when the dividend yield on the Dow reached 4.0 percent. The first counter-trend rally topped out in 1969 just below the 1966 high.

The second leg down commenced shortly thereafter and did not halt and reverse until the dividend yield reached 5.0 percent. The second counter-trend rally topped out in early 1973. Note that this counter-trend rally exceeded the 1966 and 1969 high-price areas. Coincidentally, the dividend yield on the Dow at the 1973 top was 3.0 percent. Many investors believed a new bull market was underway at this point due to the Dow eclipsing the 1966 high price. As you can see, however, the market rolled over into a third leg down, which was completed when the dividend yield on the Dow registered 6.0 percent in December, 1974.

Now let's compare the this with the current bear market.

If my analysis is accurate, the first leg down began in early 2000 and ended in October 2002. If you refer back to the Investment Quality Trends chart for the Dow in Figure 6.2 in Chapter 6, note that at the bottom of the first leg down the dividend yield was below the 3.0 percent yield area. The counter-trend rally began in earnest in 2003 as the Greenspan Fed and the Bush administration unleashed the one-two punch of extremely low interest rates and relaxed federal tax rates on capital gains and dividends.

In late 2003 through the fall of 2007, we see what happens when massive amounts of home equity, never- before-seen degrees of leverage by speculators, and institutions using lethal doses of derivatives can do to the stock market. When the Dow eclipsed its 2000 high in 2006, investors believed, just as they did in 1973, that a new bull market was underway. And, just like 1973, the market rolled over into another leg down.

The second leg down bottomed intra-day on March 9, 2009, with the dividend yield on the Dow reaching 4.90 percent, 10 basis points (10 one-hundredths of 1 percent) within 5.0 percent. Simultaneously our Blue Chip Trend Verifier recorded that 72 percent of our select blue chips were in the Undervalue category, indicating that the potential for a counter-trend rally was high.

As we know, a very powerful counter-trend rally has developed. If the pattern of this bear market mirrors that of bear markets in the past, the counter-trend rally should retrace at minimum 50 percent of the previous down leg, which would approximate 10,300 on the Dow. As you know now, counter-trend rallies can also return to the old high as in 1969, or can even breach that level as in 1973 and 2006.

Knowledge of these patterns allows investors to initiate new undervalued positions at important reversal points such as the March, 2009 lows and to recoup some lost ground on older positions that may have been held through the previous decline. If and when the counter-trend peaks and begins to decline again, it is time to take profits on overvalued stocks, place stop losses on below-rising trend stocks that have advanced significantly, and raise cash in anticipation of the next halt and reversal.

The Next Bull Market

In the case of the present cycle, I believe one more down leg remains ahead of us. When the 3.0 percent dividend-yield area on the Dow was violated in late 2008 and declined to almost 5.0 percent, it became clear to me that the era of irrational exuberance had come to an end. As such, it would be completely logical for the Dow to return to its historically repetitive extremes of undervalue and overvalue at dividend yields between 3.0 percent and 6.0 percent, respectively. At the very minimum, I would anticipate at least a retest of the March 2009 lows.

However the end game plays out, as night follows day there will be a new bull market. It should be quite profitable over its life but it will be different than bull markets of the past as the wind will no longer be at our backs. The perfect storm of low interest rates, an accommodative Fed, friendly personal and corporate tax rates, cheap money and ready liquidity, lax regulation and oversight, not to mention irrational exuberance, will be absent.

Not to worry though, because quality and value will be plentiful, which for value investors is the best environment one could hope for. Although it won't be as easy as in the past, it will be achievable. To quote the John Houseman line from the old Smith Barney commercials: "We make money the old-fashioned way. We earn it." To modify the John Houseman line from the old Smith Barney commercial; "We'll make money the old fashioned way, we'll earn it."

Value and the Stock Market

Long-time radio commentator Paul Harvey is credited with saying, "In times like these, it helps to recall that there have always been times like these." Although a little on the folksy side, Mr. Harvey does a pretty good job of hitting the nail on the head. Business, the economy, and the markets move in cycles, not in straight lines.

Investor sentiment is subject to cycles as well. When all is well in the financial world, no amount of bad news can drag the markets down. When sentiment falls, no amount of good news can move the markets higher. Intellectually, experienced investors should understand this. Emotional extremes are part of the natural order and thus are necessary, but they are also short-lived.

Cycles have a rhythm and a pattern, much like the seasons: Winter follows fall and spring follows winter, and so forth. In similar fashion, recessions follow boom times and bull markets lead into bear markets. Through it all, the world keeps spinning on its axis. According to the Dividend-Yield Theory, just as dividend-yield extremes represent historically repetitive areas of under value and overvalue in individual stocks, so, too, are there dividend-yield extremes that represent historically repetitive areas of undervalue and overvalue in the stock market.

Indeed, both the Dow Jones Industrial and Utility Averages have long established Profiles of Value, which can provide investors with invaluable information about the level of value that is present or absent in these widely followed proxies for the broad markets at any given time.

Investors who understand these cyclical patterns of dividend yield and know how to measure whether the cycle is in the early stage and offers good current value, or if the cycle is in the later stages where most of the value has been realized, have a greater probability for maximizing their real total return and minimizing their potential downside risk.

Maximizing return and minimizing risk are key for the investor whose primary investment goal is to build a pool of capital and growing income stream from that capital sufficient to fund their or someone else's cash needs.

Dividend-Yield Cycles

Volumes of books can be written about cycles because they can be observed in infinite ways. Time and space prohibit a lengthy recitation of the myriad examples, but most readers will be familiar with cyclical patterns we observe without a second thought: in agriculture, the weather, the seasons, history, politics, sports, and, of course, in human life. Some cycles are hard-wired by nature. Others are the result of the collective thoughts and actions of billions of people.

One of the central postulates of the Dividend-Yield Theory is that there is a cyclical aspect to dividend- yield patterns. Indeed, decades of stock market research has produced strong evidence that high- quality stocks with long histories of dividends and rising dividend trends generally fluctuate between repetitive extremes of high dividend yield and low dividend yield. The nexus for these fluctuations is the cyclical ebb and flow of the stock market, which is the result of market participants anticipating or reacting to news and information from the worlds of economics and politics.

Fundamental to the dividend-value strategy is that these recurring themes of yield can be used to establish envelopes of undervalued (low) andovervalued(high) price levels.

These lows and highs, which represent the bottoms and tops of cycles, are identified by simply charting the dividend yield over a sufficient period of time for the dividend-yield pattern to emerge. By calculating the repetitive dividend-yield areas where a stock or index turns down, or reverses a slide and turns up, the future behavior of that stock or index can be anticipated.

Once a dividend-yield pattern is established, the pattern tends to remain constant unless an exogenous event compels market participants to establish new parameters of undervalue and overvalue of dividend yield.

When a dividend is raised, undervalue and overvalue price limits will automatically adjust higher to maintain the historically established yield percentages. In general, the stock price will adjust accordingly to reflect the increased value as the result of the dividend increase.

The dividend-yield cycles are established by the market, which can be explained by the most basic of economic principles of the supply-and-demand theory as taught in Economics 101. When a high-quality, dividend-paying stock declines in price to the point where the dividend-yield is historically high, experienced investors with substantial amounts of capital earmarked for opportunities that represent good value begin to accumulate a position. This accumulative buying halts the decline, stabilizes the price, and begins to reverse the trend. When a price reversal in a stock becomes apparent, other investors initiate purchases and the price begins to rise.

Once a rising trend has been established and appears to have legs, less disciplined investors will begin to take positions in the stock. Almost simultaneously, investors who purchased the stock at undervalued prices become increasingly inclined to secure their profits by selling. By the time the price reaches its historic level of overvalue, the yield is no longer attractive enough to compel sufficient numbers of new buyers to take positions in the stock.

As soon as the early buyers become sellers and new buying interest evaporates, the price will begin to decline. Once a declining price trend becomes evident, the remaining stockholders will move to salvage what they can of any profits and their original principal. This wave of selling will continue until a historically high dividend yield again attracts enough new investors to halt the decline. There, at undervalue, the long-term investment cycle appears all over again. To summarize this point before we move ahead: It can be observed that dividend-paying stocks fluctuate over time within a range of low dividend yield—establishing a peak of overvalue—and high dividend yield— establishing a valley of undervalue. The peaks and valleys identify areas in which stocks should be bought or sold.

Undervalue and Overvalue Cycles

Each stock has a unique profile of undervalue and overvalue; that is, distinctive high- and low-yield characteristics, as shown in Figure 6.1. Because no two profiles are identical, each stock must be studied on an individual basis, so in addition to producing income, dividend yield can also be used as a tool to identify value in the stock market.

Depending on the primary trend of the market and economy, the average length of time for a stock to rise from undervalue to overvalue has fluctuated between three years and five and three- quarters years. Some stocks cycle at a faster pace. Other stocks, especially those with frequent dividend increases, have a long upward climb and may be held longer before a sale at overvalue is necessary. In general, the amount of time required to cycle down from overvalue, through the declining trend and back to under- value, is two years.

Bull and Bear Market Cycles

There are moments in every market cycle when investors question whether it is a bull market, a bear market, or a sideways trading range. A 200-p0int drop could just as easily be a correction in a bull market, the first break in a bear market, or the low point of the range in a sideways market. In hindsight we all have 20-20 vision, which provides little comfort at the moment clarity is most critical.

Although no one likes uncertainty, this is particularly true for investors. Benjamin Graham has said, "Individuals who cannot master their emotions are ill- suited to profit from the investment process." This is especially poignant during periods of extreme market volatility when emotions are running high, because investors will often make decisions that can undermine their ability to build long-term wealth. Throughout investment history, pearls of wisdom about the proper course of action for investors during times of market uncertainty have come from figures such as John D. Rockefeller and his now famous exhortation to "buy when the blood is running in the streets." Even the Oracle of Omaha, Warren Buffett, has weighed in with, "Be fearful when others are greedy. Be greedy when others are fearful."

The quotes from Rockefeller and Buffett may represent sound contrarian philosophy and appear simple enough, but what qualified as "blood in the streets" to John D. and "fearful and greedy" to Brother Buffett may be subject to interpretation.

When your goal is to maximize real total return and minimize risk, it may prove more prudent to leave subjective measures of analysis to the more intrepid. Instead focus on objective measures of analysis that have provided clear indications of value over significant periods of time. For this we look again to the Dividend-Yield Theory, which, when applied to the Dow Jones Industrial Average (DJIA), has provided strong and reliable signals over the last 80-plus years.

Dow Jones Industrial Average Cycles

Just as repetitive areas of good value can be established by dividend yield for individual stocks, optimum buying and selling areas have also been established for the DJIA based on its composite dividend. In Figure 6.2 there are seven charts (a-g) that provide a technical portrait of fundamental value as expressed by dividend yield extending back to 1949.

For readers who are not proficient in using charts, here are some useful tips to help you understand the information that is displayed: The vertical axis on the far left edge of the chart displays price; the horizontal axis along the bottom of the chart displays time. Because this is a monthly chart, each of the vertical lines within the chart area represents one month. The top of the line is the high price for the period, the bottom of the line is the low price for the period, and the hash mark to the right is the closing price of the period.

As discussed previously, every stock has a unique profile of undervalue and overvalue dividend yield. In the case of the DJIA, there are four distinct areas: one that represents overvalue and three that represent undervalue. Unique to the Investment Quality Trends charts are horizontal lines that represent the price levels at which specific areas of dividend yield are reached. When the dividend is increased, the line will move up to display the price for that specific level of dividend yield. When the dividend is decreased, the line will move down to reflect the price for that specific level of dividend yield.

What these charts illustrate is that four specific areas of dividend yield have a repetitive pattern: 3.0 percent at overvalue; 4.0 percent, 5.0 percent, and 6.0 percent at undervalue. Historically, the DJIA has offered good value whenever the dividend yield has risen to 6.0 per-cent, as it did in 1949-1953, 1974, and in 1978-1982. Strong price support also has been evidenced at the 4.0 percent yield level, which halted and reversed declines in 1960, 1962, 1966, 1971, and, most notably, on October 19, 1987.

A 5.0 percent yield halted and reversed a major decline in 1970. More recently, the DJIA came within 10 basis points (10 one- hundredths of 1 percent) of the 5.0 percent yield level on an intraday basis on March 9, 2009. Note that in the last chart (g), the line representing the month of March, 2009 does not accurately display just how close the dividend yield came to the 5.0 percent level. The reason for this is that the dividend for the DJIA has declined since March, which has lowered the price at which a 5.0 percent dividend yield would be realized.

With the exception of the period between 1995 and 2007 (which we will examine separately in Chapter 8), when the Dow reaches a 3.0 percent yield a Rising Trend has been reversed. This occurred in 1950, 1961, 1966, 1968, 1973, 1987, and 1990. If we were to produce a chart beginning in 1929, it would also illustrate that the dividend yield declined to just beneath the 3.0 percent level prior to the Great Crash.

So we see that all four yield areas have a significant history. With the exception of the period between 1995 and 2007, which we believe former Fed Chairman Alan Greenspan accurately identified as a time of "Irrational Exuberance," did a 3.0 percent yield fail to signal the approach of a serious market decline. When the DJIA was priced to yield 6.0 percent or more, the market offered a profitable buying opportunity.

The Dow Jones Utility Average

Just as undervalue and overvalue levels can be established for the DJIA, so, too, can they be set for the Dow Jones Utility Average (DJUA). Figure 6.3 shows the measures of the market, a feature on the front cover of every issue of Investment Quality Trends that tracks the undervalue and overvalue parameters for the DJIA and the DJUA. Note that the profile for the DJUA follows that of the DJIA closely: overvalue at a 3.0 percent dividend yield and undervalue at a 6.0 percent dividend yield.

The 4.0 percent undervalue yield for the DJIA listed in the measures of the market reflects the first area of undervalue dividend yield.

Potential to Undervalue

Low High

Price Yield 7172 4.00% Potential to Undervalue Low High

Price Yield 278 6.00%

Points %

Down Down 2372 25% Points %

Down Down 99 26%

Potential to Overvalue

High Low

Price Yield 14344 2.00% Potential to Overvalue High

Low

Price Yield 556 3.00%

Points %

Up Up 4800 50% Points %

Up Up 179 49%

Current

Annual Dividend Price Dividend Yield 9544 $286.88 3.01% Current Annual Dividend Price Dividend Yield 377 $16.67 4.42%

Value Cycles

Since the dawn of stock-market analysis, investors have searched for the one indicator that is perfect in its predictive capabilities. Although it is titillating to entertain such a notion, if such an indicator were to exist, it would eventually destroy the markets because all risk would be removed for practitioners and they would eventually own everything.

Even when investors are successful at identifying the primary trend of the market, there are stocks that rise during bear markets as well as stocks that decline during bull markets. All things being equal, I would rather know the direction of the primary trend at not, but market indicators can only tell you what the current temperature of the market is, not where to find good current value. The truth of the matter is there is the stock market and there is the market of stocks, which are two entirely different things.

We have reached that understanding after having observed our market of stocks, the Select Blue Chips, over the course of the last 40-plus years. As a result of these observations, we have developed another cyclical indicator, which measures what is always most important—values.

Our universe of Select Blue Chips is grouped into four distinct categories: Undervalued, Rising Trends, Overvalued, and, Declining Trends The Undervalued category consists of stocks that represent historically repetitive extremes of low-price and high dividend-yield.

Category Stocks Percent

Undervalued stocks 84 30.8%

Overvalued stocks 61 22.3%

Rising Trends 90 33.0%

Declining Trends 38 13.9%

273 100%

The Rising-Trend category consists of stocks whose stock price have risen at least 10 percent from its Undervalued base. The Overvalued category consists of stocks that have reached historically repetitive extremes of high price and low dividend yield. The Declining-Trend category consists of stocks whose stock price has declined at least 10 percent from its overvalued peak.

Twice each month, we calculate how many stocks are in each category and what percent that number is of the total. For over 40 years, we have tracked each category in the Investment Quality Trends "Blue-Chip Trend Verifier".

By tracking the movements between categories and comparing those movements against the highs and lows on the DJIA, we have established that whenever the percentage of stocks in the Under- valued category rises between 70 percent and 80 percent of the total, it has been coincident with a low cycle in the DJIA and many good buying opportunities. In contrast, when the percentage of stocks in the Undervalued category declines to 17 percent or less, it has been coincident with a high cycle in the DJIA, which indicates the market is Overvalued and susceptible to a major market decline.

By example, in early 1973 the DJIA eclipsed the high price established in 1966 and 1969, which many investors believed signaled the beginning of a new bull market. What many failed to take into consideration however, was that the new high was reached at the 3.0 percent dividend-yield level, which you now know represents the historically repetitive area of overvalue dividend-yield. At the same time the "Blue-Chip Trend Verifier" in the first January 1973 edition indicated there were just 17 percent of the Select Blue Chips in the Undervalued category. Shortly thereafter, the rally failed and the market declined until the bear market bottom was recorded in December 1974.

Now contrast the statistics just mentioned to January 1975. In the First-January 1975 issue, the measures of the market indicate that the dividend yield for the DJIA was 6.1 percent and the percentage of Select Blue Chips in the

Undervalued category reached 80 percent. Obviously, this was a spectacular buying opportunity. In the spring of 1987, stocks in the Undervalued category represented only 12 percent of our total universe. The dividend yield? You guessed it. Not only did it reach the 3.0 percent, overvalue area but shot through it to boot. At that juncture it was obvious the market was extremely overvalued on an historical basis. This situation was corrected thoroughly on October 19, when the DJIA registered its largest percentage drop ever in a single day.

A more contemporary example can be found in January 2000, when the DJIA peaked just below the 12,000 level. In the First- January 2000 issue, we find that only 13 percent of our Select Blue Chips were in the Undervalued category. The market slide that ensued did not end until October, 2002. Interestingly, even though the market decline was halted, in the First- November 2002 issue we find that only 16 percent of our stocks were in the Undervalued category, a clear indication that the bear market was far from over and a harbinger of what was to come five years later.

Value Still Prevails

we address cycles, indicators, and value in the market further because there are some important issues between 1995 and 2007 that must be addressed. At this juncture, however, we have learned the value of being able to identify both dividend-yield cycles and undervalue/overvalue cycles.

Knowing these cycles exist and having the means to measure them will be a tremendous help in achieving your long-term investment goals. A word of caution before we close, however; don't lose sight of the forest because of the trees. That is, don't get so caught up in following the stock market that you lose focus of the market of stocks.

Quality and Blue Chip Stocks

A value-based approach to investing such as the dividend-value strategy is a powerful arrow to have in your investment quiver. When properly implemented through high-quality companies that represent historically good value, an investor is well-armed to out-duel the competition.

The terms quality and value are repeated frequently throughout this book because they are the twin pillars on which the foundation of the dividend-value strategy rests. In previous chapters we have discussed the importance of value in a generic way; in later chapters the discussion will become much more specific.

Before we get into the finer aspects of value identification, however, it is important to introduce and understand the concept of quality and itsunderlying importance. As stated previously, the dividend-value strategy can be implemented with any company that has paid dividends long enough to establish a repetitive pattern. For optimum investment results, however, it is best implemented through high- quality, blue chip stocks.

More than 40 years of research shows that the dividend-value strategy, when implemented through high-quality stocks with long track records of excellence and performance, provides a powerful tool for building wealth. At the end of the day, it is the building of wealth, both of capital and income, to meet the present and future cash needs of the investor that is most important.

Quality and the Stock Market

The extract that follows first appeared in The Dividend Connection, Geraldine's second book written with her son, Gregory Weiss. It is so well written there is simply no way to improve upon it.

In the real estate market, quality is determined by three measures: location, location, location. Three measures can also be applied to quality in the stock market: performance, performance, performance.

1. Financial performance is the first measure of quality. This includes the company's record of earnings, dividends, debt-to-equity ratio, dividend payout ratio, book value, and cashflow.
2. Production performance is the second measure of quality. We look for a company that manufactures useful products or services and actively pursues research and development of new products or services. The company must also demonstrate an ability to market its products or services successfully.
3. Investment performance, as reflected in long-term capital gains and dividend growth, is the third measure of quality. The most important objective of an investor is a rewarding total return. A well-managed company with a strong financial performance will generate a total return that will out- perform any other investment vehicle.

These three measures of quality do not stand alone. They are intertwined in the fabric of the company and its shareholders' goals. All of our research has shown that there is as much or more profit potential in high- quality stocks than there is in stocks of inferior or unproven quality—and with far less risk.

Our method of investing in the stock market focuses exclusively on blue chip stock selection. It involves limiting investment selections to blue chip stocks and purchasing or selling those stocks based on their individual profiles of undervalue or overvalue.

CHAPTER 3

What Is a Blue Chip Stock?

As best as we can tell, there are at least 15,000 publicly traded companies in the U.S. financial markets alone. I doubt seriously that anyone would fault me for suggesting that not all of them represent blue chip stocks, let alone companies that are worthy of investment consideration.

There is a certain irony in the fact that, in a book in which we focus on value-based investing as a business as opposed to mere gambling or speculation, the objects of our affection, blue chip stocks, get their name from the highest denomination of betting chips in a poker game. Be that as it may, the term blue chip is nonetheless reserved for only the highest quality stocks. The reason for this is simple. Blue chip companies have a reputation for dependability as well as offering the best potential for increasing shareholder value through dividend growth and capital gains.

Although many blue chip companies are household names, an equal number, if not more, are not. There are also many stocks that are household names but are far from being blue chips. As you can see, it is important to have a mechanism or filter if you prefer to eliminate the pretenders from the contenders, so to speak.

Since 1966 we have used six criteria, which we call the Criteria for Select Blue Chips (our designation for the highest-quality blue chip stocks), as a starting place for our investment considerations. When a stock has passed this filter for its qualitative characteristics, we then analyze it further to determine its historically repetitive areas of under valued and over valued dividend yield.

At first glance these six criteria appear relatively simple, which they are; no rocket science here. When combined into one fundamental filter however,it effectively eliminates approximately 98 percent of the domestic publicly traded universe of stocks. To put that into further perspective, of the roughly 15,000 publicly traded companies in the U.S. markets, only 350 companies meet this criteria, and of those 350 we can establish clear cut dividend-yield profiles for only 273 companies

Company Symbol

Abbott Labs ABT Bank of New York Mellon BK

ABM Industries ABM Bank of America BAC

AFLAC AFL Bard, CR BCR

AGL Resources AGL Barnes Group B

Air Products & Chemicals APD BB&T Corp BBT

Alberto-Culver ACV Becton, Dickinson BDX

Alexander & Baldwin ALEX Bemis Company BMS

Altria Group MO Black & Decker BDK

American States Water AWR Block, H&R HRB

Ameren AEE Bob Evans Farms BOBE

American Express AXP Boeing BA

Ameron International AMN Brady Corp. BRC

Ametek AME Bristol-Myers Squibb BMY

AON Corp. AOC Brown-Forman BF.B

Apache Corp. APA Burlington Northern BNI

Apogee Enterprises APOG California Water Service CWT

Applied Industrial AIT Campbell Soup CPB Technologies Cardinal Health CAH

Aqua America WTR Carlisle Companies CSL

Archer-Daniels-Midland ADM Cass Information Systems CASS

Associated Banc-Corp ASBC Caterpillar CAT

AT&T Inc. T Century Tel Inc. CTL

Atmos Energy ATO Chevron Corp CVX

Automatic Data Processing ADP Chubb Corp CB

Avery Dennison AVY Church & Dwight CHD

Avon Products AVP Cincinnati Financial CINF

Badger Meter, Inc. BMI Cintas Corp CTAS

Baldor Electric BEZ Citigroup Inc. C

Bancorp South BXS Clarcor CLC

Bank of Hawaii BOH Cleco Corp CNL

Bank of Montreal BMO Clorox CLX

Coca-Cola KO Franklin Resources BEN

Colgate-Palmolive CL Frisch's Restaurants FRS

Comerica CMA First Midwest Bancorp FMBI

Commerce Bancshares CBSH Fulton Financial FULT

Commercial Metals CMC Gallagher, Arthur J. AJG

Community Trust Bancorp CTBI Gannett GCI

Consolidated Edison ED Gap Inc. GPS

Conagra Inc. CAG GATX Corp. GMT

Connecticut Water Service CTWS General Dynamics GD

ConocoPhillips COP General Electric GE

Consolidated Water CWCO General Mills GIS

Cooper Industries CBE Genuine Parts GPC

Curtiss-Wright CW Gorman Rupp GRC

CVS Caremark Corp CVS Graco Inc. GGG

Deere & Co. DE Grainger, WW GWW

Diebold Inc. DBD Granite Construction GVA

Disney-Walt DIS Greif, Inc. GEF

Dominion Resources D Hancock Holdings HBHC

Donaldson Company DCI Harris Corp. HRS

Dover Corp. DOV Harsco Corp. HSC

DPL Inc. DPL Hasbro Inc. HAS

Eaton Corp. ETN Heinz, H J HNZ

Eaton Vance EV Henry, (Jack) & Associates JKHY

Ecolab Inc. ECL Hershey Foods HSY

Emerson Electric EMR Hewlett-Packard HPQ

Enbridge Inc. ENB HNI Corp. HNI

Energen Corp. EGN Home Depot, The HD

Ennis Inc. EBF Hormel Foods HRL

Equifax Inc. EFX Hubbell Inc Class B HUB.B

Equitable (EQT) Corp. EQT Huntington Bancshares HBAN

Exelon Corp. EXC International Business IBM Exxon Mobil XOM Machines

Family Dollar Stores FDO Illinois Tool Works ITW

Federal REIT FRT Imperial Oil Ltd. IMO

Fifth Third Bank FITB Independent Bank Corp IBCP

First Merchants Corp. FRME Ingersoll-Rand Plc IR

FirstEnergy Corp. FE Integrys Energy TEG

Florida Public Utilities FPU International Flavors & IFF

FPL Group FPL Fragrances

Johnson & Johnson JNJ Northrop Grumman Corp. NOC

Johnson Controls JCI NSTAR NST

Kaydon Corp. KDN Occidental Petroleum OXY

Kellogg K OGE Energy OGE

Kimberly-Clark KMB Old National Bancorp ONB

LaClede Group LG Omnicom Group OMC

Legg Mason LM ONEOK, Inc. OKE

Limited Brands LTD Otter Tail Power OTTR

Lincoln Electric Holdings LECO Overseas Shipholding OSG

Lincoln National LNC Group

Lockheed Martin LMT Owens & Minor OMI

Lowe's Companies LOW Paccar Industries PCAR

Lufkin Industries LUFK Parker-Hannifin PH

M&T Bank MTB Pentair Inc. PNR

Marriott International MAR Peoples Bancorp PEBO

Marsh & McLennan MMC PepsiCo PEP Companies Pfizer Inc. PFE

Marshall & Ilsley MI Philip Morris International PM

McCormick MKC Inc.

McDonald's MCD Piedmont Natural Gas PNY

McGraw Hill MHP Pitney Bowes PBI

MDU Resources MDU PNC Financial Group PNC

Medtronic Inc. MDT Polaris Industries PII

Merck & Company MRK PPG Industries Inc. PPG

Meredith Corp. MDP Procter & Gamble PG

MGE Energy MGEE Protective Life PL

Middlesex Water Co. MSEX Public Service Enterprise PEG

3 M Company MMM Group

Mine Safety Appliances MSA Pulte Homes Inc. PHM

Molson Coors Brewing TAP Questar Corp. STR

MTS Systems MTSC Raven Industries RAVN

Northwest Natural Gas NWN Raymond James Financial RJF

National Fuel Gas NFG Regal Beloit RBC

New Jersey Resources NJR Reliance Steel & RS

Nike Inc Cl B NKE

Noble Energy Inc. NBL

Nordson Corp. NDSN

Nordstrom JWN

Norfolk Southern Corp. NSC

Northern Trust NTRS Aluminum

RLI Corp. RLI

Rockwell Automation ROK

Rollins Inc. ROL

Roper Industries ROP

Royal Bank of Canada RY

Ruddick Corp. RDK

Schering-Plough SGP

Schlumberger Ltd. SLB Selective Insurance Group

SIGI Sempra Energy SRE

Sensient Technology SXT

Sherwin Williams SHW

Sigma-Aldrich SIAL

Smith, A. O. AOS

Smucker, JM SJM

Snap-On Inc. SNA

Sonoco Products SON

South Jersey Industries SJI

Southern Company SO

Southwest Bancorp OKSB

Stanley Works, The SWK

State Street Corp STT

Stepan Company SCL

Sterling Bancorp STL

Sunoco Inc. SUN

SunTrust Banks STI

Supervalu Inc. SVU

Torchmark Corp. TMK

Toro Co. TTC

Travelers Companies, The TRV

TrustCo Bank Corp. NY TRST

Trustmark Corp. TRMK

UGI Corp. UGI

Union Pacific Corp. UNP

United Technologies UTX

Universal Corp. UVV

Valley National Bank VLY

Valmont Industries VMI

Valspar Corp. VAL

VF Corp. VFC

Vulcan Materials VMC

Walgreen Co. WAG

Wal-Mart Stores WMT

Washington Post WPO

Washington Federal WFSL

Washington REIT WRE

Watsco Inc. WSO

Weingarten Realty WRI

Wells Fargo & Company WFC

Susquehanna Bancshares SUSQ

Synovus Financial SNV

Westamerica Bancorporation

WABC

Sysco Corp. SYY

T. Rowe Price TROW

Target Corp. TGT

TCF Financial TCB

Teleflex Inc. TFX

TJX Companies TJX

Weyco Group WEYS

WGL Holdings WGL

Whirlpool WHR

Wilmington Trust WL

Wisconsin Energy Corp WEC

Zions Bancorp ZION

The Criteria for Select Blue Chips

Most stock analysis is conducted through two central disciplines: fundamental and technical. Fundamental analysis has two main subsets: the quantitative and the qualitative.Quantitativegenerally refers to numbers, things that can be measured—earnings, divi- dends, cashflow, payout, debt, and so forth.Qualitativegenerally refers to intangibles— characteristics that can't necessarily be meas- ured but nonetheless are important; for example, name recognition such as a company's brand, management expertise, commitment to research and development, industry cycles, and so forth.

Technical analysis is considered by many to be the polar opposite of fundamental analysis. Whereas fundamental analysis involves analyzing the economic characteristics of a company in order to estimate its value, technicians are primarily interested in price movements because the fundamentals, they believe, have been fully factored into the price. Another definition would be the study of supply and demand in a stock or market to determine what direction, or trend, will continue in the future.

Generally, but not always, analysts tend to favor one discipline over the other. For many practitioners, there is simply no way for the two disciplines to co-exist.

Our approach is based on a combination of the two disciplines, what we call a fundamental approach to technical analysis. The Criteria for Select Blue Chips is how we identify fundamental quality, or what stocks to buy. Our Profiles of Value, the study and identification of the historically repetitive patterns of undervalue and overvalue areas of dividend yield, is how we identify value, or when to buy, sell, or hold.

In later chapters we will discuss undervalue and overvalue in much greater detail. Before we can begin to focus on the when, however, we first have to identify the what. That is the primary purpose of the Criteria for Select Blue Chips—to identify corporate excellence, or quality.

Dividend Increases and Earnings Improvement

Criteria 1 and 6 earlier both reference 12 years: dividend increases in five of the last 12 years, and earnings improvement in seven of the last 12 years. One of the most frequent questions I am asked is what is so special about 12 years?

The average business/economic cycle lasts approximately four years. Over the course of 12 years, then, the economy and markets will go through three complete cycles. During that period, a company will experience the inevitable economic surprise, be it on a macro level, which affects all companies, or on a micro level, which is specific to that company, industry, or sector. There is an equally high probability for major legislative and/or tax changes that will require a period of adjustment. In short, adversity is part of the cost of doing business. As such, a consistent track record for earnings growth is not only difficult to achieve, but also to sustain over significant periods of time.

For a company to meet both of these criteria, their earnings and dividends must show consistent improvement. Steady and improving earnings and dividend performance over the course of 12 years is not luck; it is evidence of strong and capable management. The list of Select Blue Chips that have achieved consistent earnings and dividend growth is quite extensive. Only those from the Undervalued category in the mid-September, 2009, are listed below

Company Symbol Company Symbol

Abbott Laboratories ABT

AFLAC AFL

International Business Machines

IBM

Altria Group MO

Archer-Daniels-Midland ADM Automatic Data Processing ADP Bank of Hawaii BOH

Bank of Montreal BMO

Becton, Dickinson BDX

Boeing BA

Cardinal Health CAH

Caterpillar CAT

Johnson & Johnson JNJ

Kimberly-Clark KMB

Lockheed Martin LMT

M&T Bank MTB

McDonald's MCD

Meredith Corp. MDP

Mine Safety Appliances MSA

Nike, Inc Class B NKE

Noble Energy Inc. NBL

CenturyTel CTL

Chevron CVX

Overseas Shipholding Group OSG

Cincinnati Financial CINF PepsiCo Inc. PEP

Cintas Corp CTAS Philip Morris International PM

Clorox CLX Polaris Industries PII

Coca-Cola KO Procter & Gamble PG

Colgate-Palmolive CL Raymond James Financial RJF

Community Trust Bancorp CTBI Sigma-Aldrich SIAL

ConocoPhillips COP Sysco Corp. SYY

CVS Caremark Corp. CVS Target Corp. TGT

Eaton Vance EV Teleflex Inc. TFX

Exelon Corp. EXC TJX Companies TJX

Gallagher, Arthur J. AJG Trustmark Corp. TRMK

Greif, Inc. GEF United Technologies UTX

Harris Corp. HRS Valspar Corp. VAL

Hasbro Inc. HAS VF Corp. VFC

Henry, Jack JKHY Walgreen Company WAG

HNI Corp. HNI Wal-Mart Stores WMT

Home Depot, The HD Weyco Group WEYS

The most reliable measure of good management is long-term performance, a proven ability to grow the net earnings of its company and maintain a rising trend of increased dividends. You work hard to save the capital you put to work in the markets. Don't entrust it to just any company; put it to work with the best. The proof, once again, is in the pudding.

S&P Quality Ranking in the "A" Category Standard & Poor's has provided Earnings and Dividend Rankings, commonly referred to as Quality Rankings, on common stocks since 1956.

Dividend Truth

According to Standard & Poor's:

The Quality Rankings System attempts to capture the growth and stability of earnings and dividends record in a single symbol. In assessing Quality Rankings, Standard & Poor's recognizes that earnings and dividend performance is the end result of the interplay of various factors such as products and industry position, corporate resources, and financial policy. Over the long run, the record of earnings and dividend performance has a considerable bearing on the relative quality of stocks. The rankings, however, do not profess to reflect all of the factors, tangible or intangible, that bear on stock quality.

The rankings are generated by a computerized system and are based on per-share earnings and dividend records of the most recent 10 years—a period long enough to measure significant secular growth, capture indications of basic change in trend as they develop, encompass the full peak-to-peak range of the business cycle, and include a bull and a bear market. Basic scores are computed for earnings and dividends, and then adjusted as indicated by a set of predetermined modifiers for change in the rate of growth, stability within longterm trends,and cyclicality. Adjusted scores for earnings and dividends are then combined to yield a final ranking.

The Standard & Poor's Earnings and Dividend Rankings for Common Stocks are as follows:

A+ Highest B+ Average C Lowest

A High B Below average D In reorganization A Above average C Lower NR

A ranking of NR signifies no ranking or insufficient data because the stock in not amenable to the ranking process.

For inclusion in the universe of Select Blue Chips, a company must initially have at minimum an A Quality Ranking. The company may remain in the roster if its Quality Ranking declines to a B , but will be removed from the listing if it is downgraded further.

At Least Five Million Shares Outstanding

There is an extensive body of research on the impact that market capitalization, or cap size, exerts on the returns of stocks. As a result of this research, the mutual fund complex has designed and offers a multitude of funds that invest solely in one capitalization segment of the market. These funds are easily identifiable as the term Cap will be part of the fund name. By example: Mega Cap, Large-Cap, Mid-Cap, Small-Cap, Micro-Cap, and so forth.

Also common today, particularly among financial consultants, is to provide their clients who invest in individual stocks the ever- ubiquitous pie chart, to show what percentage of their holdings fall into the various capitalization segments.

For many, this type of analysis is sacrosanct. So be it; it is not within the purview of this book to engage in that debate. For our purposes of identifying quality, we aren't overly concerned with market capitalization. What we do care desperately about though is liquidity. With enough common shares outstanding, a stock is assured of liquidity; we never want to be in the position of having to make an appointment to buy or sell a stock. Institutional investors, whose importance to our method is outlined in the next section, prefer to invest in companies that are liquid so they can establish large investment positions without disturbing the price of the stock. Equally important is that when the time comes to sell, they want to know that there will be sufficient numbers of buyers. Few experiences are as frustrating as trying to buy or sell a large position in a thinly traded stock. For institutional investors who frequently deal in large sums of capital, an orderly entrance and exit are extremely important. Lastly, liquidity helps to guard against share price manipulation.

At Least 80 Institutional Investors

When we use the term institutional investor,we are referring to the vast number of mutual funds, Exchange Traded Funds (ETFs), hedge funds, banks, insurance companies, pension fund and retirement companies, major brokerages, and money managers. On any given trading day, these groups account for the vast majority of trading activity. As such, their collective buying and selling decisions will exert an enormous impact on the trend of stock prices. In other words, institutions are the 800-pound gorillas of Wall Street.

Whether they choose to acknowledge it or not, institutional investors can exhibit some fairly predictable behavior. This is due, in no small part, to the fact that it is a closely linked community. This is to say that they associate with, listen to, and behave like other institutional investors. As value investors, we can use this propensity for like-minded behavior to our advantage.

It is not uncommon when using the dividend-value strategy to be early to the table, which means that we often take positions in high- quality companies that offer excellent historic value long before other investors. Eventually one or two institutional analysts will stumble upon one of our companies, write up a buy recommendation, and distribute it to its traders or sales force.

Nothing in the institutional community remains secret very long, so when the word gets out, the full force that is institutional buying power kicks in. Strong institutional buying eventually hits the radar screens of our favorite investor type, the momentum investor. In simple terms, a momentum investor attempts to capture capital gains by buying a stock with a discernible uptrend in price, or to short a stock with a discernible downtrend in price. The underlying belief is that, once a trend has been established, it is likely to continue in that direction than to move against the trend.

There is nothing intrinsically wrong with this idea. In fact, we engage in some momentum investing ourselves. There is nothing more attractive than a high- quality company with an undervalue price, a high-yield and upward momentum in its dividend trend.

Okay, we're not really momentum investors, but I think you get the point.

To bring this point to conclusion, between institutional interest and momentum investing, stocks that we purchased at excellent historic value will often reach their historic upside potential, at which point we lock in our profits and search for another high-quality undervalued opportunity.

Of the six Criteria for Select Blue Chips, the number of institutional sponsors is the least rigid, which is to say there is nothing magical about the number 80. What is important is evidence of widespread interest in a stock, and that it has attracted a broad and diverse institutional following. In terms of price stability, we prefer to find that 80 or more institutions hold 50 percent of the common shares outstanding, rather than one or several institutions holding the same amount; with diversity comes an element of safety. Most full- service brokers and investor databases can provide information on the number of institutional investors and their percentage of holdings in any individual stock.

At Least 25 Years of Uninterrupted Dividends

Of the six criteria that comprise the Criteria for Select Blue Chips, this is the one that separates the big dogs in the tall grass from the pups in the weeds. We are often asked if there is really a meaningful difference between a company that has paid uninterrupted dividends for 25 years and one with 10, 15, or 20. The short answer is absolutely.

In a sufficient number of instances, our research indicates there is a greater likelihood for price volatility and less reliability in the trends of earnings and dividends for companies with shorter track records of uninterrupted dividend payments.

Although we lack a single empirical measurement that explains this phenomenon, our best guess, based on our experience, is that the market, which posseses all the wisdom from its collective participants, has determined that companies that have achieved this milestone have earned elite status and investors simply treat them differently.

What we do know is that over a 25-year period a company will go through many business and economic cycles,willexperience the exhilaration of bull markets and the despondence of bear markets, will see their products or services enjoy periods of wide popularity and periods of less; the list can go on and on.

In the final analysis I believe it all boils down to one factor, namely, competence. If a company can weather the myriad challenges it will inevitably face over such a period of time and maintain a strong record of earnings growth and maintain a rising dividend trend, that is competence. If a company can keep its products and services at the forefront of consumer interest, or reinvent itself if necessary, that is competence. If a company can consistently attract, train, and retain the next generation of management that will continue a tradition of excellence—that is competence.

You work hard to save the investment capital you put to work in the financial markets. All things being equal, who are you most comfortable associating with that capital? For us the answer is easy: the most competent companies we can find.

With the rare exception, the majority of the current 273 companies in the Investment Quality Trends roster of Select Blue Chips have paid uninterrupted dividends for 25 years.

The Importance of Dividends

At this juncture the importance of cash dividends should be crystal clear. When a dividend is increased, the stock price will inevitably rise to reflect the increase in value. Conversely, when a dividend is reduced, the stock price will inevitably decline to reflect the decrease in value.

Dividends are an indicator of value and a predictor of future growth, which attracts new investors to the company and provides a tangible reward for accepting investment risk. Value-conscious investors can depend on cash dividends to either provide a reliable stream of income to meet their current cash needs or as capital to reinvest to keep pace with inflation and improve their standard of living. A company that pays cash dividends year after year and increases those dividends regularly is well managed.

An ongoing dividend stream is the most reliable evidence a company is generating sufficient earnings to cover expenses, pay the interest on its debt, grow the company, and reward its owners. When a dividend is increased, the stock owner knows without reading a balance sheet or an annual report that their company is performing.

There Is No Profitable Substitute for Quality

we have explored the importance of quality as it pertains to the dividend-value strategy. Although the strategy can be implemented through any stock that has paid dividends long enough to establish a discernible pattern for repetitive areas of undervalue and overvalue, four-plus decades of research has proven that for the best investments results, investors should confine their investment considerations to only the highest-quality, blue chip stocks.

High quality, blue chip stocks are the first to rise in a bull market and the last stocks to fall when the market declines. In good times, blue chip companies outperform both their lesser competitors and the economy. In bad times, they resist adversity best. Time and time again, experience has shown, there is no profitable substitute for quality.

Although quality is one of the twin pillars of the dividend-value strategy, it isn't the final word;valueis. In the following chapters, we discuss the importance of identifying value to build a winning portfolio.

Value and Blue Chip Stocks

Recognizing quality is an essential component of the dividend- value strategy, but quality and value are entirely different measurements. The Select Blue Chips listed within the pages of Investment Quality Trends are all high-quality companies, but not all of them represent current good value. That is, even the highest- quality stock can be overpriced. Accordingly, once investors have established the qualitative bonafides for a blue chip stock, the measures of good value should be applied to maximize both the safety of capital and the potential for real total return.

Finding Good Value

If I had to choose just one factor as the key to investment success, it would be the ability to recognize and appreciate good value, which leads to two important questions: How is value measured in the stock market, and how does an investor know when the price of a stock represents good value?

There are three fundamental tools that investors use to establish value in the stock market: dividend yield, price-earnings ratio (P/E), and price-book value ratio (P/B) Of the three measures, the primary measure of value in the stock market is the receipt of dividends, which is expressed as dividend yield. Dividend yield cuts to the chase; when all else is stripped from the bone it is the dividend yield that reveals the true value of a company's stock.

This is not to suggest that price-to-earnings (P/E) ratios or price-to-book-value (PB) ratios are unimportant. As primary measures of value, both ratios are less than perfect; however, as confirmation measures for the value the dividend represents, both can be quite useful.

Price-Earnings Ratio

The price-earnings or P/E ratio is probably the first analytical tool most investors learn about because it is the most commonly used measure of value. In brief, the ratio expresses the stock's price in relation to the company's trailing 12-month earnings. The ratio is calculated by dividing the earnings per share into the price of the stock. The resulting figure produces a ratio of the price to the earnings.

By example, if a company's trailing 12-month earnings are $1.95 per share and the current stock price is $24 per share, by dividing $1.95 into $24, the result is 12.30, which we round down to 12. When expressed as a ratio we would say the P/E is 12 to 1. Depending on current economic and market conditions, 12 to 1 could be high, low, or somewhere in the middle.

When earnings, stock prices, and interest rates are depressed, as they typically are in a bear market, it is not uncommon for P/E ratios to fall into the single digits. Conversely, when earnings, stock prices, and interest rates are robust, as they typically are during periods of expansion, it is not uncommon for P/E ratios to rise well into the teens and twenties.

In general, depending on the overall growth rate within any stock industry group, any ratio below 15 to 1 is believed to represent fair value. In like fashion, a P/E ratio above 20 to

1 suggests that the stock price may be overvalued. However, stocks have their own personali¬ties, and a high P/E ratio for one stock may be an acceptable ratio, depending on the company's growth characteristics. The market will also often grant higher valuations to a particular stock or industry that captures its fancy. Our personal preference as a firm is a P/E ratio that is closer to 10 to 1.

As you can tell, there is a certain amount of subjectivity when it comes to P/E ratios, another reason why identifying the repetitive extremes of under value and over value dividend yield is so important.

Price-Book Value Ratio

In accounting terms, book value is all of a company's tangible assets (what you can see and touch), minus debt, minus preferred stock, and minus intangible assets (such as patents and goodwill). For normal people, book value is what is left if the company were to go out of business, liquidate all of its assets, and pay off all its debts. This figure is then divided by the total common shares outstanding to determine the book value per share.

The P/B ratio compares the market's valuation of a company (price per share) to the value indicated on its financial statements (book value per share). By example, if a company's stock price is $20 per share and the most recent book value is $10 per share, by dividing $20 by $10 the result is 2. When expressed as a ratio we would say the P/B is 2 to 1.

When the P/B ratio is one (1 to 1), it means the market value is in sync with what the company is reporting on its financial statement. When the ratio is greater than one, it means the market is willing to pay a premium above what the company reports on its financial statements. When the ratio is less than one, it can mean one of two things: The market is nervous about the value of the company and is unwilling to pay full price, or investors have incorrectly valued the stock.

For some analysts, to question the validity of book values is to commit heresy. For the truly objective analyst, however, it is difficult to overlook the obvious deficiencies in book values for making accurate valuations. For one, how assets and liabilities are valued leaves room for creative interpretation, as we have discovered recently with financial companies. Another is that some companies, such as those in the technology and service sectors, have hidden (intangible) assets such as intellectual property that are of great value, but are not reflected in the book value. Lastly, most accounting procedures fail to account for the effects of inflation on asset prices. Book value figures, therefore, can just as easily be understated as overstated.

Even the great Benjamin Graham, whose work I credit for much of my academic/intellectual development, and whose favorite measure for value identification was book values, cautioned investors that a stock does not necessarily represent good value simply because it can be purchased at or close to book value. In his book The Intelligent Investor, Graham advises investors to be cognizant, too, of the price the market is placing on shares, to know how many dollars are on hand for each dollar of short term debt, and to know that the dividend is well protected.

As is the case with earnings and the P/E ratio, book values and the P/B ratio cannot be dismissed. They are important measures of value as they can confirm the message of the dividend-yield trend.

Dividend Yield

We believe that the most important measure of investment value is the dividend yield. We believe this to be true because of three factors:

1. Dividends are the result of earnings.
2. A rising dividend trend is a predictor of growth.
3. Repetitive dividend-yield extremes establish reliable areas for undervalue and overvalue prices.

Enlightened investors have learned there is generally one catalyst—higher earnings or management's reasoned expectations for higher earnings—that justifies a dividend increase. Think about it. No management, particularly that of a blue chip company, wants to suffer the public embarrassment of a bad call. Before the decision to raise a dividend is made, then, management has to believe the prospects for improved earnings, now as well into the future, must be strong. No manager with a lick of sense will raise the dividend if there is any doubt about future earnings.

Throughout this book, you will read the terms undervalue and overvalue. In our lexicon, these are historically repetitive extremes of low-price/high-yield and high-price/low-yield, which we call Profiles of Value. There is no one Profile of Value that can be applied to every stock. Each stock has it unique Profile of Value that must be analyzed and evaluated individually.

The Bluest of the Blue Chips

Even among blue chips, some stocks are more blue chip than others. These are stocks that have both an A+ quality ranking and the Investment Quality Trends"G" designation. A stock is awarded the "G" designation when the company achieves average annual dividend growth of 10 percent or greater over the past 12 years.

Company Symbol

Archer-Daniels-Midland ADM

Automatic Data Processing ADP

Caterpillar, Inc. CAT

Cintas, Corp. CTAS

Colgate-Palmolive CL

CVS Caremark Corp. CVS

Jack Henry & Associates JKHY

Nike, Inc. Class B NKE

PepsiCo, Inc. PEP

Philip Morris International PM

Sigma-Aldrich SIAL

Sysco Corp. SYY

Target Corp. TGT

TJX Companies TJX

United Technologies UTX

Walgreen Company WAG

Wal-Mart Stores, Inc. WMT

Figure 5.2 Royal Blue Chips—Highest Investment Quality (A+)

The Faded Blues

The Select Blue Chips listed in Investment Quality Trends are an elite representation of the highest-quality publicly traded companies in America. Achieving Select Blue Chip status is not a one-time event, however; the designation must be continuously earned.

For varying reasons, more than 100 stocks have been deleted from our blue-chip-stock list over the last 44 years. Many were deleted because they were acquired by another company, some because they eliminated their dividend. On occasion, a Select Blue Chip can run into temporary or cyclical difficulties and their S&P Quality Ranking may be downgraded to "B," which signifies below-average quality. Even if they meet the five remaining criteria, we feel compelled to delete the stock from our blue chip roster and transfer it to our list of faded blues.

They will be eligible for blue chip reinstatement if their quality rankings return to "B+"(above average) or cure other criteria deficiencies.

Back to Basics

It has been said that an investor can find whatever he is looking for in the stock market. If questioned, most investors will tell you they want to make money. Although all investors like to make money, some are really interested in the excitement or being entertained. Others, believe it or not, use the stock market to work out deep-rooted psychological issues. Some simply want to commiserate with their friends or neighbors about how the stock market stuck it to them again and there is no way the little guy can beat the big boys at their game.

Investing is a business, and most businesses that are successful are the result of the owner's willingness to do things that others don't want to do or won't do. Accordingly, identifying high-quality stocks that represent historical good value and giving them time to reach their full potential may not appeal to the investor looking for fireworks and immediate gratification. However, patience, in the stock market, is indeed a virtue.

In 1974, Geraldine conducted an interview with Benjamin Graham, which was later published in what at the time was theSan Diego Union. In that interview Graham offered an interesting perspective on the value of patience:

It's hard enough to find good values. When a stock rises slowly, intrinsic value can keep pace with the gradual increase in the price of the stock. However, when the price escalates quickly, faster than the fundamental development of the company, then the stock must be sold and a new investment decision made. Every new investment decision bears the risk of being a mistake.

Although the approach outlined in this book may not be entertaining or exciting enough for some, for the serious investor whose goal is developing wealth to meet his current and future cash needs, the dividend- value strategy has delivered time and again over the course of the last 40-plus years. For the enlightened investor, the growth of wealth is sufficient award to make patience well worth the effort.

Now that you know how to identify quality and value, we can turn our attention to understanding how cycles and trends impact both stocks and the stock market.

AVOIDING LOCAL RISK

Investment in shares is inherently a risky business since the company may go bankrupt, rendering the shares worthless. More frequently, the company may go through a spell of poor profitability, reducing dividends and thence the share price.

There are two types of risk associated with investment in company shares, specific risk and market risk.

Specific risk/alpha risk

Also known as alpha risk, specific risk is associated with the individual risk inherent in holding shares in individual companies. There is absolutely no reason to endure specific risk, since it can be alleviated by buying a spread of companies across several market sectors. The usual rule given is to hold around 20 (at least ten) different stocks. It is not necessary for them to be in 20 different market sectors, but they should certainly be in ten or more sectors. Mathematical calculations show that 90 percent of the risk of holding individual shares can be lost by holding a portfolio of just ten shares; 95 per cent of risk with 20 shares.

A good example of the consequence of specific risk was seen in 1999 when the UK retail sector fell out of favour and share prices dropped heavily. A well-diversified portfolio would have been only slightly troubled by this, and shares held in other sectors might well have gained as money removed from the retail sector was reinvested (pushing up prices) in other sectors.

If you cannot afford to own ten or more shares, the same spread of risk can be obtained through investment in a pooled fund such as a unit trust.

Market risk/beta risk

Market risk reflects the fact that all the market may drop together, as in a crash or a bear market. There is no way of avoiding this except by hoping that things will get better again in time. Or, if you were lucky, by selling everything before the fall became noticeable. The difficulty then is that you might sell up only to find that the fall was purely temporary.

A risk associated with a market fall is the so-called beta risk. When markets change direction, some shares traditionally change in the same direction to an exaggerated extent. Thus if the market falls by ten per cent, some individual stocks will fall by only five per cent, and others by 20 percent. This difference relative to the market represents the beta risk of the share, and it is possible to buy large tables of beta risks for all shares. High beta risk stocks should be sold if you think the market is about to fall, or bought if the market is about to rise.

Penny shares have high beta risks, unit trusts have low beta risks. It is important to remember that the tables of beta risk were compiled on the basis of past experience, which may not recur in the future.

There has been some debate about the accuracy of beta values. A new model by Ross, 'Arbitrage Pricing Theory' (APT), seeks to subdivide beta risk into the following components:

- inflation
- industrial production
- investors' liking for risk
- interest rates.

Returns are assessed from the sensitivity of a share to each component.

Risk and marketability

Do not confuse alpha and beta risks with alpha and beta ratings of marketability.

OVERSEAS INVESTMENTS

It is not necessary to restrict your investments only to the UK market and there are many foreign stock exchanges to choose from. Interestingly, the London Stock Exchange, sometimes known as the International Stock Exchange, is the world's largest single exchange in terms of turnover.

The world's biggest markets, in terms of capitalisation, are those of the USA and Japan. The UK is third and other large markets

Investing in Stocks & Shares

include West Germany, Italy, Australia, Hong Kong and Canada. After an agreement between the electronic trading arms of both stock markets, it is now much easier and cheaper to trade shares between Britain and the USA. A British investor pays no stamp duty or VAT on purchases, but a US levy of 0.03% on all sales (as well as broker's commission).

So-called 'emerging markets' form part of overseas investments.

Advantages

The advantages of investing overseas are principally centred on the spread of risk and reducing your exposure to the vagaries of your own economy and government. You may also be able to benefit from currency movements, which can also be listed under disadvantages!

Disadvantages

One big disadvantage is the expense of investing overseas as many brokers have high handling charges and require large minimum investments. However, it is easy enough to invest overseas through pooled funds such as unit trusts (see Pooled Funds on page 79).

The London Stock Exchange has introduced an 'Integrated Retail Service' that deals in international shares. Prices are quoted in Sterling, and currently the shares of over 300 companies are quoted. Charges to the broker are the same as those for British shares, but the broker can charge the customer any fee.

Those who hold foreign shares can seek to avoid double taxation with countries with which there are tax treaties. For example, if tax at the rate of 25 per cent has been withheld on a foreign dividend, but the tax treaty with the UK allows a tax of 15 per cent, the difference can be claimed back from the (British) Inland Revenue. Investors require form N-8BEN to make a claim from the Inland Revenue. However, these claims are complicated since they have to offset the 10 percent tax credit that might otherwise be claimed. Moreover, you may also need to file a foreign tax return too. The complication of holding foreign shares directly probably exceeds the benefit.

Another serious problem is that of currency exposure. When you invest in the UK, all the profits come directly to you. If you invest overseas, then a rise in the value of the pound sterling against the local currency may completely offset a large profit in local terms. Conversely, a stationary foreign economy may still give you huge returns if the pound falls in value. The UK investor who places his money abroad is, in effect, betting that the pound will fall, or at worst hold steady, against the local currency. It is a sad but observable fact that the pound does show a steady downwards drift against other major currencies, as it has done throughout the last 100 years.

Finally, for the direct investor, there remains the problem of converting dividends received in foreign currencies into sterling. The minimum commission exacted by the converting bank is now around seven pounds, which may easily be more than the value of the dividend! However, foreign currency cash funds managed in the UK will often be pleased to take dividends in that foreign currency at no extra charge. Nevertheless, in the short term, foreign investment involves a high degree of currency speculation by the investor, broadly expressed as a hope that the pound will fall against the foreign currency. From 1999 the effect of the new Euro has also to be considered.

Pressure selling

While on the subject of overseas markets, the reader's attention is drawn to the fraudulent activities of some foreign-based high- pressure share salesmen. These individuals, formerly operating largely from the Netherlands, but more recently for brief periods from any safe haven before the local police track them down, attempt to sell you 'bargains' in little known shares trading on the world's minor stock exchanges, often over the telephone. Never, ever buy shares over the telephone from a 'cold-caller'. Even when the shares exist at all, they have very poor marketability. Many of these fraudsters use accommodation addresses in the UK or within the EU, provide British or European phone numbers (which are re-directed further afield), and possess plausible websites, all to give them a spurious air of authenticity. Several international efforts are being made to crack down on these conmen.

A common trick is to send the investor a list of 'tips' on reliable companies, but with special emphasis on one dud company. This will be the one which is pushed as the conman's 'star tip'.

POOLED FUNDS

One well established way of spreading specific risk is to invest in a pooled fund. The money of many small investors is pooled and invested in a sufficient spread of shares, each investor having a share of the total fund. In the USA, it is quite common for groups, or clubs, of investors to join together to do this pooling of funds, and stocks are selected by mutual agreement or even with a pin! The great attraction of this method is that there are no management charges involved. Such schemes are rare in the UK, doubtless owing to the small percentage (relative to the USA) of the UK population which actively invests in shares. The Pro Share organisation (address at back of book) will provide details on how to set up your own investors' club.

Pension funds, insurance groups and similar organisations also invest funds on a pooled scale for the benefit of their depositors. However, the performance and probity of different fund managers may vary, so it is vitally important to spread investments in pooled funds among several different managers.

There are two principal schemes for pooled investment open to the small investor in the UK. These are unit trusts/OEICS and investment trusts.

Unit trusts

Unit trusts (known as mutual funds in the USA) are true trusts, with trustees, and are regulated by a government department. The trusts are open-ended funds: units are created whenever an investor wants to buy some, and are destroyed when the investor sells them back. Thus the unit trust manager is forever having to buy and sell the component shares of the trust in the market to meet the demand of investors. There are limitations imposed by the trustees on the investments which a unit trust manager can make, and the investor has no say in what the manager does. Until very recent legislation, no unit trust was allowed to borrow money to invest in shares.

Unit trusts are freely and extensively advertised in the newspapers and elsewhere. Management charges vary, but are frequently quite high, typically a 5-6 percent offer-to-bid spread and 1-1.5 percent management fee. The offer-to-bid spread is the difference between the prices quoted to the investor to buy units (the trust's 'offer' price) and to sell units (the trust's 'bid' price); managers can now choose to abolish the spread. The management fee is levied on the total market value of the shares of the trust, and is therefore deducted from the trust's dividend income. What income remains is distributed to the unit holders.

It is apparent from the foregoing that in a bear market the unit trust managers' incomes will take a knock. Many managers have a nasty habit of raising their management rate (say from 1 percent to 1.5 percent) to compensate for this. The last person to suffer from a market collapse is always the trust manager. It is also believed that pure unit trust managers tend to show a better performance overall than unit trusts managed by, eg, life insurance companies, the reason being that the pure funds do not have to pay enormous commissions to door-to-door salesmen.

When too many investors sell units simultaneously, the managers must sell their best shares quickly to pay the investors. The residual investors are left with the unsaleable rubbish. For this reason, unit trusts are unpopular with professional investors.

Open-ended investment companies (OEICs/ICVCs/UCITS) OEICs are intermediate between unit trusts and investment trusts, and are much more popular in Europe than in the UK. They became eligible as PEP/ISA investments in 1995.

OEICs are open-ended funds but, like investment trusts, are covered by company law rather than trust law. Their tax regime is similar to that of unit trusts, but there can be many types of share. There is one price for buyers and sellers (no bid-offer spread), so management charges may be higher instead.

When investors sell units in open-ended funds (eg unit trusts and OEICs), the funds have to sell their underlying shares. If too many investors sell too much at once, the fund will be a forced seller of too many shares, obtaining poor prices. In order to protect the remaining investors in the fund, a dilution levy is charged to those selling out.

The many share types make for easy switching between funds. One OEIC can have, for example, shares in an equity fund, shares in a bond fund and shares in a cash fund.

Investment trusts (ITs)

Investment trusts are not really trusts at all and the oldest (Foreign & Colonial) predates the unit trust industry by many decades, having been founded in 1868.

They are companies which invest in other companies' shares. Like all companies, investment trusts are not permitted to advertise except in full-scale share prospectuses. However, they are permitted to advertise their savings schemes. The investor in an investment trust can vote on its strategy and can buy its shares on the stock market as for any other company, with the same charges.

Investment trusts are closed end funds. The funds under their control are not affected by the purchase or sale of investment trust shares. Instead the price of the shares of the investment trust rises to reflect their increased demand. Shares trade at a premium or, more commonly, at a discount, to the underlying value of the shares in which the trust is itself invested.

This offers the potential to an investor to buy a share in an investment trust for, let us say, £1 and thereby to own pooled shares worth £1.20, a common occurrence with ITs and a problem which makes them vulnerable to large predators. A large company may offer £1.10 to buy your own pound share, and sell the underlying assets for their full value of £1.20, although it is of course necessary for a majority of shareholders to agree to this.

The Financial Times newspaper now publishes daily the discount (or premium) for each investment trust, using data supplied by Fundamental Data Ltd. This information is computed from published dealings by the trusts, and has been shown to be usually very accurate (to within 1-2 per cent) when the trusts publish their own figures at six-monthly intervals.

Investment trusts are also able to buy any stock they want, subject to shareholders' approval, and can borrow money to invest in shares. If the new shares rise in value faster than the cost of the interest charges on the borrowings, then the trust gains considerably in value. This procedure is known as gearing (or, occasionally, as leverage). It is a practice indulged in at times by most investors in other contexts. Buying your own home with borrowed money represents gearing. You would not do it if you thought the value of the house in 25 years' time would be less than the money you had paid back in capital and interest.

Naturally, if the newly acquired shares do not rise fast enough in value to cover interest charges, then the trust will lose money at an unusually fast rate. An illustrative case of this was seen with the Govett Strategic Investment Trust after the 1987 crash, when the trust sold stock rapidly at a depressed price to repay its high borrowings as quickly as possible. Govett Strategic's share price tumbled to about 50 per cent of its pre¬crash level, against an average market fall of 30 per cent.

The charges of investment trusts are quite modest relative to unit trusts. A broker's normal buying and selling charges will amount to around 5 per cent altogether, ie inclusive of both buying and selling, while management charges are normally less than one per cent of the total fund - often much less for the larger trusts.

The great attraction of investment trusts is their savings schemes (available now for most of the larger ones). Here the investor can save a regular amount every month, re-invest dividends from the trust and make occasional lump sum purchases. The total buying charges in these schemes rarely exceed 0.5 per cent, and may be as low as 0.3 per cent (excluding any stamp duty payable) of the value of the shares purchased. Selling the shares often needs to be done through a bank or broker and is therefore more expensive, but a few trusts offer very cheap selling arrangements too.

Investment trusts have a clear cost advantage over unit trusts through their savings schemes and lower annual charges. Moreover, their long term average performance is better than that of unit trusts, except after a steep market fall

So why are investment trusts not better known? The answer is twofold. Like all quoted companies, investment trusts are not permitted to advertise themselves, and most of them pay no commission to 'independent' advisors. There was recently a major 'ITs' advertising campaign on television to improve the public's awareness of investment trusts.

The reader's attention is drawn to the variety of different shares available from certain types of so- called 'split capital' investment trusts. These fill special investment niches, are not applicable to the investment strategy.

Pooled funds overseas

Unit trusts and investment trusts provide ideal vehicles for investment overseas, although the warnings given previously about overseas investments and currency movements still apply. With luck, their fund managers, often based in the foreign market, will know what they are about and all the changes in investment will be made in the local currency.

One problem to consider is whether the trust should remain fully invested in a market which the manager expects will perform badly, or should the trust sell its shares and hold cash for a while until things improve (and if so, should the cash be held locally, or in sterling)? Different fund managers have different views on this, so it is necessary to check whether the fund's strategy fits in with your own views.

The small investor in a trust invested overseas must decide whether he will make the decisions about moving in and out of a fully-invested overseas fund, or stay permanently in a fund from which the managers are permitted to disinvest into cash as they think appropriate.

Management performance of pooled funds

Tables of management performance is widely available for both unit and investment trusts, the latter being mostly members of the Association of Investment Companies (AIC), which publishes many tables of data, including monthly in its own publication.

Experience shows that few fund managers are consistently able to maintain a good performance in each and every year. It is certainly wiser to stick with the best and longest established names, who have reputations to protect.

Management charges may now be deducted from fund income (as was always the case) or from the fund's capital. Deduction from capital provides a higher yield to the investor at the expense of fund growth, and is not suited to long-term investors with no current need for income.

Beware unprincipled fund managers

The fund itself has directors or trustees who will appoint a fund manager, usually one of the institutions. The fund manager may appoint one or more individuals, or a team, to decide on the fund's investments, often subject to controls set by the fund's mandate or by its directors.

Both the fund manager, and those individuals who personally make the decisions, receive bonuses to the extent that their investment performance exceeds that of the fund's 'benchmark' - how well the fund should have performed had it followed some kind of fixed rule (such as investing only in the shares of the FTSE 100 index). A key factor that may affect management decisions is that bonuses, once paid, never have to be repaid.

There is potential here for a conflict of interests, since some fund managers may be inclined to take reckless risks to out-perform (equals large bonus), but not have to repay the bonus when long- term performance suffers as a result of these unwarranted risks. This distortion may be particularly noticeable among those who run the so-called 'hedge funds', since the hedge fund managers typically receive enormous bonuses for out-performance - sometimes as much as 20 percent of the fund's gains. By their nature, hedge funds are supposed to reach limited investment goals with limited exposure to risk, for example by running a fund comprising a mixture of shares, bonds, cash and derivatives. However, in a rising stock market, its managers may be very tempted to buy bucket-loads of shares so as to out-perform their mandate and secure for themselves a large bonus. If the rising market suddenly collapses, innocent investors would find that their supposedly hedged fund actually comprised largely shares that were falling steeply in value. For four years the managers pay themselves enormous bonuses for out-performance, despite the fact that they are breaking their mandate. In the fifth year the stock market suffers a reversal, the investors are faced with unexpected large losses (since the fund lacks its intended cushion of cash and bonds), but the managers do not have to repay their bonuses. Usually the fund just goes into voluntary liquidation instead, as investors quit.

Another way in which some fund managers can cheat their funds (and their customers) is to take on large borrowings to invest in a rising stock market. It is obvious that, if you can borrow money at five per cent to invest in shares gaining ten per cent from the stock market, then you must make more money than another fund manager of equal talent who does not borrow money. Out- performance equals larger bonus.

At the end of the market rise, you sell some of the newly purchased shares to repay the debt, and keep the profit for the fund.

There is nothing wrong with this procedure of itself, since both the investors and the fund managers stand to profit. Indeed, the ability of investment trusts to borrow, whereas generally unit trusts do not, partly explains the out-performance of the former over the latter over many years. The other reason for the superiority of the investment trust over the unit trust lies in its generally lower management charges, enforced by an independent board.

The problem with using borrowings to enhance performance comes when the managers become too greedy, and start to take on too much debt at excessive interest rates for many years - sometimes decades.

The present managers are creating a long-term problem of debt and interest for their successors. It is hard to understand why the independent boards of some investment trusts have ever allowed this potentially disastrous practice. Today, after investment returns have been reduced in line with inflation, but the heavy debt burden remains, few boards of investment trusts will permit new long-term borrowings, and have frequently repaid the excesses of the past. Certainly it is desirable to invest only in investment trusts that lack the legacy of enormous and expensive long-term borrowings. Check the level of the trust's debt in its annual report before investing.

There is another unsavoury aspect of the desire of some fund managers to secure their bonuses. The recent easy availability of very cheap money has enabled many privately-funded venture groups (PFVs) to make takeover offers for good companies that are well backed with surplus cash, surplus money in their pension funds or, especially, with large holdings of freehold land; these companies have nevertheless for some reason been neglected by the stock- market. Usually the problem is that the company has a cash deficit, or is in a declining business. Let us suppose that the target company has a current share price of 8op per share. The PFV makes an offer, heavily funded by cheap debt, to buy the shares for loop each. This represents an easy profit for the fund managers that currently hold shares in the large company, so they are likely to sell the shares uncritically - and anticipate their enlarged bonuses.

The company so treated will now be 'rationalised'; that is, shrunk until the remaining parts are profitable, and the spare cash/land/ pension surplus will be used in part to repay some of the debt assumed by the PFV. The remainder of the spare cash will be used to pay a large 'special dividend' to the lucky new owners. After three years or so, the revitalised company without its spare assets will be offered again for sale to the stockmarket for, typically, about £3 per share. The sales pitch will emphasise that this formerly loss-making concern is now profitable, and the sale proceeds will be used to repay the remaining debt of the PFV and to provide a very healthy profit to its owners. Meanwhile, the original fund managers will be among those who have paid £3 to acquire a stake in a diminished asset that they once held in full for £1 (or 8op). And they do not have to return their bonuses for this crass (or cynical) misjudgement.

There has been a strong outcry amongst various expert financial commentators against the gullibility and greed of the institutions, with the result that the PFVs are not finding it so easy today to work this kind of profitable turn-around.

Tax advantages of pooled funds

Unit and investment trusts also have tax advantages over individual investments by a private investor. If the latter keeps buying and selling shares, he will soon run into the capital gains exemption limit on capital gains. The trusts have no such problem and can buy or sell as often as they like without incurring Capital Gains Tax. The holder of the trusts only incurs his tax liability when he sells the units or investment trust shares, and he only incurs tax on his gain on the original investment, not on all the transactions carried out by the trust.

Fund of funds

The ultimate in pooled funds is the 'Fund of Funds', a class of unit trust which invests the money of its investors in other unit or investment trusts, usually on a global basis.

This provides the extreme in spread of risk for small investors, unless there is a world-wide collapse of shares (not unknown). However, not only do the original unit trust managers make a charge, but so do the Fund of Fund managers. This double imposition ensures below-average performance, since such a wide spread of shares is nearly certain to match the average performance of global share prices - before the charges. Indeed, it is possible that the managers of one of the subsidiary funds may be selling a stock while the managers of another subsidiary are buying it!

Not recommended, then, except for the very small investor who wants an exceptional spread of risk.

Off-shore funds

Off-shore funds, such as some unit trusts, do have certain tax advantages, especially to expatriates working overseas. UK residents will have to pay Capital Gains Tax after selling their units regardless of whether the fund is off-shore or UK based, unless they emigrate first. Moreover, switching between different off-shore funds, which was once possible free from UK tax, also became liable to Capital Gains Tax after April 1989. Favoured off-shore investment havens include Luxembourg, Liechtenstein, Bermuda and the Channel Islands.

One stated reason to use off-shore tax havens is to defer paying tax from a high rate today to a lower rate later. The obvious disadvantage of the funds is their inaccessibility if something goes wrong - remember Barlow Clowes? If you must invest in this way, and there is little benefit if you are a permanent UK resident, be sure to use one of the large, well-respected fund management groups with an off-shore branch.

Ethical trusts

A number of unit trusts have been launched specialising in ethical investments only. These trusts, depending on their stated degree of ethicality, avoid investment in any or all of stocks associated with armaments, tobacco, whale products or anything else which offends liberal views.

These are new trusts and, during the great bull market of the 1980s, their general performance was acclaimed as being as good as those of the non-ethical unit trusts. Less is heard of the investment merits of ethical trusts today. It is likely that they will always under perform the ordinary trusts in the long term, since the latter can always make the same investments as the ethical trusts, while the ethical trusts will always miss out on booms in non-ethical sectors. 'Green' trusts invest exclusively in companies that are environ¬mentally friendly.

Purchase of unit trusts

Unit trusts are widely advertised in newspapers, and if you clip out and fill in a form, then you have agreed to accept the contract of purchase.

If, however, you have bought a unit trust stake through a salesman who came to your home, then you currently have 7-14 days to 'cool off' before the contract is legally enforceable. There is no 'cooling off' period for purchases of unit trusts made in most other ways, nor for purchases of investment trusts. The exception is for purchases within an ISA scheme when the cooling off period is currently seven days.

Timing of unit trust purchases

One of the biggest problems for those who market unit trusts to investors is that they are always at their most popular just after a large market rise, ie at the top of a bull market when they are most likely to fall, rather than after a market crash or in a bear market when prices are probably cheap. There are whole generations of would-be investors who buy unit trusts just before a crash, then, disillusioned, sell out after the crash, thereby ending their chance of getting their money back when the markets rise again.

The Institutions

The institutions are those large companies which invest huge sums of money, usually pooled money, in the shares of the Stock Exchange, as well as in other investments. The institutions include pension funds, insurance funds and unit and investment trusts.

The buying and selling power of the institutions completely dominates the market. Private investment has been a declining force as a proportion of the market share throughout the last 100 years. This decline has quickened since 1945 as successive governments have made private investment decreasingly tax-efficient relative to ownership of housing, pensions and, until recently, life assurance. The recent huge privatisation issues by the Conservative government were intended to broaden the base of private share ownership. However, studies have shown that few of the buyers of such stocks have gone on to become active investors in other companies.

Today, private investors hold fewer than 20 per cent of the shares traded on the UK stock market. This may sound like a large voting block and so it would be if the shares were all in a few hands. But two pension fund managers can put their heads together to swing, say, ten per cent of a vote at the company's annual meeting. To achieve a counter-balancing vote in the opposite direction might require some 3000 private investors to collude together.

Because the dominance of the institutions is so great, there is no point in trying to buck their views. If all the institutions have decided to sell stock today, then it is simply futile to buy stock until the fall has been arrested no matter how wrong the institutions may be on fundamental grounds.

A good example of this occurred on the third day of the October 1987 stock market crash when, after two days of price falls, many private investors reckoned the market was oversold and plunged in. They were probably right, but the institutions swamped the market with more selling of stock as prices rose, and down went the share prices to new lows again.

The Zero Sum Game

A zero sum game is one in which there must always be as many equal winners as there are equal losers. Chess is a zero sum game, darts is not since here the ratio of winning margin of winner to loser may vary.

The dominance of the institutions on the stock market makes investment in stocks effectively a zero sum game for them. For every institution that performs well, another must do badly since the contribution of the private investor is negligible.

The consequence is that the institutions as a whole cannot perform better than the relevant indices of stock movement. In fact, on average they under perform the index by an amount equal to their costs of buying and selling shares.

It follows inevitably that anyone who can match the index perfectly will outperform more than 50 per cent of the institutions who, let it be remembered, include the unit and investment trusts.

It may be that some fund management groups can often outperform the FTSE or All-Share indices, but experience shows that very few do so on a consistent basis. Moreover, a good manager tends to move around from fund to fund, so that even a good trust may do badly after his departure.

To be sure, there are some good fund managers around with better records than most (M&G and Fidelity come to mind), but the zero sum game ensures that the average unit trust will slightly under perform the market and charge the investor a large fee for the privilege.

Fund managers like to run lots of unit trusts, partly because it offers lots of choice on the 'washing powder' principle (the more types of washing powders you sell, the greater the chance someone will pick your powder and not that of the competition), but also because, by the law of averages, some trusts are bound to perform better than average and can be heavily marketed. The less successful funds are kept hidden until, by a lucky chance, their turn at the head of the performance lists comes around.

The problem of consistent underperformance is well recognised by the unit trust industry, and one attempted solution has been the launch of index-linked funds. As the name suggests, these funds are designed purely to track the relevant indices of share movements, and their performance will always exactly equal the zero sum average performance in terms of unit price performance. Several trusts now compete on their low charges.

Examples include those managed by Virgin and Legal & General.

However, once again the fund manager will take his cut, so that the income which the investor will receive is certain to be less than he would have received had he invested directly in the stocks of the index himself. Perhaps the primary attraction of the index-linked fund is to ensure average performance from money invested overseas. One or two investment trusts provide index-linked performance, for example the Edinburgh UK Tracker Trust.

The main problem with an investment in a tracker fund is that it must, by definition, follow a falling index all the way down. By contrast, an active fund manager can move some or all of the share holdings into cash. Thus, index trackers tend to out-perform active fund managers when the market rises, and under-perform when the market falls.

CERTIFICATES OR NOMINEE ACCOUNT?

All investors today have to make the decision whether they prefer to hold shares themselves in certificated form, or to let a broker or a fund manager hold the shares for them in 'nominee accounts'. By law, shares held in a nominee account are actually owned by the broker or fund manager, although the investor retains 'beneficial ownership'. The nominee investor is therefore entitled to the proceeds (eg dividends) from the investment, while the nominee operator receives the company accounts and any perks. The reader should note especially that whereas the Financial Services' Compensation Scheme pays out up to £48,000 compensation per shareholding if the stockbroker goes bankrupt while carrying out share- dealing transactions, the maximum total payout per investor is £48,000 for all the shareholdings together held in the same stockbroker's nominee account.

Some companies have been prevailed upon to make their perks (such as cheap shopping) and accounts available to nominee investors, but a few, most notably the shipping line P&O with its well-known ferry fare concessions on some types of stock, make the perk available only to direct investors. P&O was taken over in 2006, and the perk was lost.

The advantages of direct shareholding are therefore manifest. Less obvious are the advantages of being a nominee holder; typically, fewer worries about where to store the share certificate, often cheaper dealing and, allegedly, less paperwork (my experience is that the investor receives a deluge of statements instead).

Of course, an investor can choose to hold some shares directly and others in a nominee account. For example, in 2007 all ISAs must be held as nominee accounts.

A third option is to become a direct electronic shareholder through Crest, and this will be discussed below.

Many brokers put a limit on the total sum which can be owed to them within an account by private investors. Some even limit the maximum expenditure on any one transaction.

THE BROKER

Choosing a broker

There are several ways of buying shares.

- Directly from the company when it makes an Offer for Sale with a prospectus in the newspapers. This is particularly the case with government privatisations. If your offer is accepted, you will receive a Letter of Acceptance - see example on page 94.
- Directly from a unit trust group, who advertise extensively in the newspapers. Alternatively you can buy shares in an investment trust through the trust's savings scheme.
- Through a bank, accountant or solicitor. Unfortunately, all these parties may want their cut. Also they may have an infuriating habit of demanding cash from you instantly when you buy stock, while paying you much later when you sell.
- Through the stockbroker arm of your bank, if it has one (not to be confused with dealing through your bank manager).
- By becoming a client of Barclays Stockbrokers Ltd which, as well as having its own large client lists, also took over the popular Charles Schwab/Sharelink telephone operation in January 2003. This makes it the largest stockbroker for private clients in the UK, and its address and telephone number are given under 'Useful Addresses'. Its charges are moderate for dealing by telephone with certificates, or by phone or the Internet for nominee accounts, and you can trade in American and many other foreign shares. You will not, however, be able to seek advice from this basic dealing operation. Barclays Stockbrokers also operates other accounts for those requiring further stock- broking services.

- By joining one of the number of cut-rate 'dealing only' services, such as those of 'Share-Dealing' (Halifax plc). Halifax uses nominee accounts to save paperwork so you do not receive the actual share certificate, which is held by Halifax on your behalf.
- The government is encouraging the introduction of Share Shops, retail outlets which deal in shares. There are very few of these at present, but a number of banks and building societies have expressed interest.

A good example is the National Westminster Bank's 'touch-screen' dealing system installed in many of their larger branches.

ALLOTMENT LETTER No. ABC-123

This document is of value and is negotiable until 3pm on 25th April 200X. If you are in any doubt as to the action you should take or if prior to receiving it you have sold all or part of your holding of ordinary shares in the company, you should take personal financial advice from your stockbroker or other professional advisor immediately.

The Council of the Stock Exchange has agreed to admit to the Official List the new Ordinary Shares which are now being issued. It is expected that dealings will commence on 1st April 20 0X.

NEWSTORES plc

(Registered in England - No. 345678)

LETTER OF ACCEPTANCE

SIR PATRICK BIJOU

Mr. ANTHONY INVESTOR OF NO FIXED ABODE LONDON
AB1 9ZY

Dear Applicant(s) 15th March 200X

1. Your application to buy shares in Newstores plc has been accepted for the number of shares shown above. If this is less than you applied for, a cheque is attached for the difference.
2. General Information (in very small print).
3. Instructions for renunciation and registration, splitting and consolidation (in very small print).

Yours sincerely,

Chairman

Sales and purchases of a selected range of shares can be made on the spot and settled for immediate cash, provided that you take the share certificate and identification in with you.

- An off-market transfer of shares, for example between friends, requires a 'stock transfer form' to be completed and sent to the registrar. These forms can be obtained from legal stationers. One of the principal publishers of these forms, Oyez, is listed under Useful Addresses. An example form is shown on pages 96-97. Until the abolition of stamp duty, it will be necessary for Stock Transfer forms to be stamped, for which 0.5 per cent of the value of the shares is charged (at the rate of £5 for every £1,000 of shares, rounded up). This can be done by sending the form and a cheque to your local Stamp Office (not a post office!). The address of the local stamp office can be found in Appendix 20.

However, certain exemptions from stamp duty are permitted and these are stated on the reverse of the stock transfer form. In particular, transfers at no cost between a husband and wife are free from stamp duty. Curiously, some, but not all, of the letters of acceptance of government privatisations could be traded through the Stock Exchange, but not privately, without incurring stamp duty for a few months after the letters had been sent out.

- Applying to become a private client of a stock broking firm. This is much the most flexible option.

The London stockbrokers have very high overheads, so they are often interested only in clients with £200,000 or more to invest.

On the other hand, provincial stockbrokers, of which there are several chains, regard private clients as their bread and butter and in any case have a superior reputation for attention to private clients. Pick one out of your telephone directory and ask to be a client. Make sure that the broker is a member of the London (International) Stock Exchange, which has a partial protection scheme for clients in the unlikely event that the broker goes bankrupt in the course of a transaction.

The broker will send an application form and will probably ask for a banker's reference.

It is almost a maxim that the average member of the public stands in awe of the stockbroker. Remember that he needs you much more than you need him. There are always plenty of alternatives if he does not like you - or vice-versa.

Typical broker's commissions are set at 1.65 per cent for each transaction, whether you buy or sell. The transactions are also known as bargains. There is typically a minimum charge to be paid of £30. In addition, a broker's levy for compliance with Stock Exchange Regulations of about £5 may be charged and an Exchange levy of £1 for bargains in excess of £10,000, plus stamp duty. Stamp duty is 50p per £100 (rounded upwards) for shares purchased through Crest, but since 1 October 1999 has been increased to £5 per £1,000 (rounded up) for all other share transactions. This includes transactions between the owner of shares and a nominee account. Stamp duty applies only to purchases of shares, not to sales. Some brokers require you to maintain nominee accounts (ISAs also require this). It means that the broker retains the share certificate, but it is written in their records as though it belonged to you. More commonly though, the broker sends the share certificate directly to you, although many months may have elapsed since you bought the stock. The purveyors of nominee accounts claim that it reduces paperwork and expense for them, and saves the client from receiving the paperwork. Nominee accounts are dealt with in more detail below. Your attention is drawn particularly to the section on the potential for fraud.

Finally, many brokers will require you to settle your first share purchase with cash by return of post, before entrusting you with the Crest system.

TAURUS/CREST

Taurus

Taurus was the name given to the Stock Exchange's proposed system for paperless share ownership.

Instead of holding a share certificate, the investor would find that his share holding had become a computer entry in a nominee account.

Taurus was a project begun in the mid 1980s, but was put to one side during the government-promoted package of reforms introduced in 1986 and known as 'Big Bang'. However, work on Taurus subsequently was set in motion again and it was planned to introduce the system in 1991. Numerous teething problems finally caused its cancellation in mid-1993.

Crest

In its place, the Bank of England instituted a system of paperless trading known as Crest.

The effects of Crest are these:

Electronic settlement system

Crest is an electronic settlement system matching trades against payments and informing the company's registrars. Items already handled by the 'Talisman' Stock Exchange system are excluded. Crest does not handle takeovers and rights issues.

- Changes in costs

The advantage of Crest is that removal of much of the paper- work makes share dealing cheaper for the stockbroker. However, the brokers have to pay for the huge costs of computerisation, and this represents a flat-rate burden on all share-dealing, regardless of size. Alternatively, the broker may levy a fixed yearly fee for maintaining a nominee account for the investor. Consequently, the net effect to private investors is likely to be that charges from brokers will rise.

- Broker nominees

Private investors can elect to be nominees of their own stockbroker. This will enable them to benefit from the cheaper costs of trading with Crest, which may cancel out the increase in other broker charges. Nominee accounts should be kept separate from the broker's own affairs so that bankruptcy, or other disasters affecting the broker, ought not to affect the nominee accounts. There is, however, no certain way of ensuring that the broker has actually placed anything in the nominee account.

- The potential for fraud

A number of frauds came to light in the early 1990s when it was revealed that shares supposedly held in nominee accounts did not exist at all. The investor was just being sent a yearly slip of paper purporting to show that he held stocks which had not been bought. The potential for fraud in this area is immense, and there appears to be little proposed by way of controls on the sponsors of nominee accounts. The reader is warned to select his broker very carefully. Some large brokers now provide huge insurance cover against most risks. Check the cover with your broker.

- Voluntary use

No one is obliged to use the Crest system, unlike the compulsory use of its Taurus predecessor. Those who insist on retaining paper certificates are permitted to do so, although they are likely to find that they have to pay higher dealing costs. Private transactions, without the intermediacy of the Stock Exchange, are still possible using a standard stock transfer form.

- Effect of Crest on settlement

A 'rolling system' of settlement was introduced to the London stock market in 1994, in anticipation of Crest becoming operational. Previously, purchases and sales of shares were settled about twice a month; now all settlements were to be made within ten working days. In 1995, this was reduced to five working days, and in 2000 to three working days with most companies signed up for Crest registration.

It is evident that it will be difficult for a private investor to send a share certificate or cleared cash payment to his broker within three days. At present, many stockbrokers are allowing clients and broker to settle within ten days, with no penalty to either side. It is likely that charges for such slow settlement must rise eventually.

A side effect of the need for accelerated settlement was that the registration of shares had to be steeply accelerated from its previous lethargic state. There was a major consolidation of the registrars in 1995-96, as many felt that they could not justify the cost of improved registration procedures. Another side effect has been that there is less cash chasing shares when transactions have to be settled quickly.

- Sponsored membership

Investors who deal frequently may benefit from becoming a sponsored member of Crest (sponsored by their broker or a bank), and thereby becoming able to deal directly through Crest without having to use a nominee account. Crest Co charges the broker £10 per annum per investor for this service; brokers may pass on any charge they like to the investor. The London

Stock Exchange can now be the sponsor for private individuals with Crest at 'competitive rates'.

It is at present impossible to say how popular this service will become. Most investors who seldom trade will probably be better advised to retain share certificates - at any rate until the dust settles.

- Bonds too

It is now possible to trade most types of bond through Crest.

- Alternative electronic systems

It has been pointed out that the best electronic solution to paperless trading would be to register all share certificates on one giant computer. However, this proposal has met with fierce

Dealing in Shares 101

opposition from all those who make a living as company registrars (principally the clearing banks).

- Other countries

Numerous other countries now use fully electronic registration of share holdings. A good local example is France.

- Experience with Crest

Take up of Crest membership by individuals has been very poor since it was first introduced in 1997. Most private investors prefer the security of personally holding share certificates, rather than having to pay expensive nominee charges to a broker who can't even be bothered to send the company reports. Thus all- electronic share dealing has failed to take off in the UK. There are currently (2007) proposals by the Stock Exchange that those who hold share certificates might consider transferring to an electronic share account just like that used by the successful overseas electronic accounts rejected previously in the UK as impractical. If this occurs, all broker-sponsored nominee accounts are likely to be abandoned by most investors immediately.

New electronic system (late 2006)

A consultation between the Treasury and various interested parties in 2006 agreed that paper certificates ought to be phased out ('dematerialised') and replaced by electronic trading, probably with the investor holding a secure PIN as the password for dealing. Details at the time of writing are still very sketchy, but the dematerialisation is unlikely to occur before 2008. Shareholders would receive paper statements of their electronic entitlement held on the company's share register. It is also expected that share¬holders in nominee accounts will be able to opt-in to receive the company accounts and other announcements, but perks for nominee shareholders will remain at the discretion of the company.

Dealing services

Many brokers offer three types of dealing service:

- The dealing-only service will accept and execute your orders only, without proffering advice. Barclays Stockbrokers is such a service. The dealing-only service is normally the cheapest.
- The advisory service is more expensive and the broker will, on request, offer advice on a proposed transaction. A special, more expensive, variant of the advisory service is available from some brokers, who will volunteer advice on investments without being asked. The investor usually needs a great deal of money to qualify for this treatment.
- The discretionary service also requires a substantial minimum outlay by the investor and permits the broker to switch investments on his behalf without consultation. This service has laid itself open to the charge of 'churning', where a broker keeps trading his clients' shares unnecessarily in order to boost his own commission. Some of the more reputable brokers avoid this suspicion by charging a flat rate (at a high price) for their discretionary portfolios, regardless of the number of deals. Others enrol new clients in the broker's own unit trust. The latter entails quite high charges (like a normal unit trust), but means that the portfolio can be traded around without the individual investors incurring Capital

Gains Tax on their transactions. This is clearly beneficial to most investors.

A SUMMARY OF CHARGES

A summary of typical charges by different types of agent for share investment is given below. It used to be the case that VAT had to be paid on stock broking commissions, but this was ended in 1990. The abolition of VAT caused a small increase in commissions, since the brokers were no longer able to obtain interest on VAT payments received by them but not yet passed on.

Through broker

Commission normally 1.65 per cent, minimum £30 plus stamp duty (0.5 per cent on purchases only) plus broker's compliance levy up to £5 and PTM levy of £1 on bargains in excess of £10,000. Also market maker's 'spread' (1-10 per cent, depending on market- ability).

Through unit trust manager

Manager's spread of bid-offer normally 5-6 per cent plus annual fees (1-2 per cent of trust value).

Through investment trust savings scheme

Buying: commission 0.2-0.5 per cent plus other fees as for broker's commission. Selling: normally as for broker's commission.

COUNTRYWIDE STOCK BROKING LIMITED

(Incorporating Country, Town and Co.)

SIR PATRICK BIJOU

1-4 Broker Street, Thames Valley, TV1 9SB Telephone: 0123-987654

Branches in: Birmingham, Dundee, Edinburgh, Littlemarch-under-Water, London, Manchester, Swansea

Registered Office: Countrywide House, Hampstead, London NW1 9XX Registered in England No. 1234567

VAT Registration No. 123 4567 89

Regulated by the Financial Services Authority.

Member of the London Stock Exchange

MR. ANTHONY INVESTOR OF NO FIXED ABODE LONDON AB1 9ZY

Bargain Date and Tax Point Security Client Contract Ref. Settlement Date

O6FEB0X

+0123456

W12345D

A98765

10FEB0X

WE THANK YOU FOR YOUR INSTRUCTIONS AND HAVE BOUGHT ON YOUR BEHALF AS AGENTS

MEGASTORES ORD 25P

Time Quantity Price Consideration

13:55 1000 1.97 £1970.00

TRANSFER STAMP (N) COMMISSION

V.A.T. EXEMPT

COMPLIANCE CHARGE £1970.00

10.00

32.51

NIL

5.00

TOTAL

£2017.51

Subject to the Rules and Regulations of the Stock Exchange including any temporary regulations made by or under the authority of the Council of the Stock Exchange.

E. & O.E. V.A.T. Invoice for services rendered (N) = Not subject to V.A.T. Please retain this document for Capital Gains Tax and V.A.T. purposes.

Barclays Stockbrokers (see Useful Addresses)

Commission 1.5 per cent to £15,000 (0.85 per cent above £15,000), minimum £25 plus other fees as for broker's commission.

Bank or building society

Current charges for share-dealing are typically: (NatWest Stock- brokers Ltd, Tel: 0870 6004080) - Commission 1.0

per cent (lower above £5,000), minimum £15, plus flat rate fee of £15 for dealing in certificates, plus other fees as for broker's commission. Special, cheaper charges for government privatisation issues.

Several building societies offer special dealing rates for handling the sale of government privatisation issues. The general dealing services once offered by a number of societies have mostly been discontinued.

Discount broker

Brokers who provide an 'execution-only' service, and normally hold all their clients' shares as nominee accounts.

Example: Halifax Share-Dealing. Tel: 08457 225525. Commission minimum £15, maximum £40 for deals up to £60,000 plus other fees as for broker's commission.

Company plan

Some companies employ agents to provide very cheap dealing services in the company shares.

Example: Rio Tinto dealing through Hoare Govett Corporate Finance Ltd. Commission 1 per cent per £100, no minimum plus other fees as for broker's commission.

The Mechanics Of Share Dealing

Appoint an agent

For most share dealing, you will need a broker. The Stock Exchange (see Useful Addresses) will provide, in addition to several useful booklets about investment generally, a list of brokers prepared to deal for small private clients. Provincial brokers will usually be cheaper and have a reputation for being more approachable. See page 95 for more details.

Ensure that the broker is regulated by the Financial Services Authority (FSA), which has a compensation fund. This will reimburse most, or all, of the loss suffered by private clients in the unlikely event of a broker going out of business before a transaction is completed. Some brokers are also well insured against losses.

For investment in the savings schemes of an investment trust, write directly to the trust's managers asking for an application form for the scheme. A list of trust managers and their addresses can be obtained from the AIC, address in 'Useful Addresses'.

Buying shares

Suppose you want to buy shares in a company XYZ whose middle price in today's paper is 105 pence.

- Phone the broker (ask for him by name), then give your name and probably your account number.
- Ask 'What price is XYZ?' The broker will reply something on the lines of 'Buying price 110p, selling price 100p', or even just '100-110p'.
- If you don't like the current buying price (110p), just say 'too much' or 'not interested' and there is no further obligation.
- Otherwise, give your order such as 'buy one thousand XYZ at maximum 110p'. It is strongly advisable to state a maximum price (buying) or a

minimum price (selling). Never say 'at best'! However, you might be willing to say 'at maximum 113p'.

Get the broker to repeat this order to you, especially if you are placing several orders at once, otherwise embarrassment could be caused.

Virtually all brokers now tape-record their telephone calls.

- That ends the transaction.
- Say 'goodbye' and ring off.
- Once you have rung off, you cannot change your mind.

You should receive the Contract Note the next day. It will state exactly what has been done for you by the broker, giving the full price including details of the commission, stamp duty (where appropriate) and the Stock Exchange levy. Check that the details agree with what you wanted, complain if they do not.

Later, you will receive a statement, listing all your transactions and requiring settlement by the stated day. You write out a cheque, make it payable to the broking firm (not to the individual broker) and post it off with your client number or other form of identification so as to arrive before the stated day. It is necessary to take action to ensure that you have cleared funds in the bank in time to meet the cheque. If you normally keep the money in a building society, it will have to be transferred to your bank account in good time.

Owing to a number of frauds perpetrated on cheques 'lost' in the post, the Cheques Act (1992) provided that cheques crossed 'A/C Payee only' could only be paid to the bank account of the named individual or company. Since 2006 it is necessary to put personal identification (such as your name, account number or both) onto any cheque to be paid to a financial institution including a bank or building society.

Important - purchases of gilts and traded options must be settled on the next working day after purchase. Unless you live next door to the broker, this requires that you leave a sufficient sum on deposit with the broker before making the purchase. Some brokers will allow late settlement of gilts - ie within ten days - for a slightly higher purchase price.

In order to purchase shares in an investment trust through its savings scheme, it is necessary only to fill in the form and send a cheque. Make sure this will arrive in good time before the day, usually at the end of the month, that the trust buys the shares on the open market.

Retain all the contract notes for possible inspection by the Inland Revenue. Keep old notes for seven years. After weeks or months, your broker or the investment trust will send to you the Share Certificate. You were, however, the owner of the shares as soon as you bought them and have a full entitlement to any dividends which they paid after that date (but see page 67 for shares sold 'cum' and 'ex' dividend).

Nationality declaration

A number of companies have charters which limit the extent to which non-British citizens can buy their shares. Typical are several of the de-nationalised industries, such as Rolls-Royce and British Aerospace. The government deemed that these strategic industries should not be subject to foreign control.

Investors seeking to buy shares in these companies will be required to state that they have British nationality before the change in ownership is registered. Investors unable to make the declaration may or may not be able to complete the transaction, depending on the proportion of foreign-held shares already registered. Companies exacting this requirement from their investors tend to

CERTIFICATE NUMBER TRANSFER NUMBER DATE OF REGISTRATION NUMBER OF SHARES AB001001 0001234 20MAY0X — 1000 — ORDINARY SHARES OF 25 p EACH MEGASTORES plc

(Incorporated under the Companies Act 1948)

THIS IS TO CERTIFY THAT

MR ANTHONY INVESTOR OF NO FIXED ABODE

LONDON AB1 9ZY

is/are the registered holders of **ONE THOUSAND** ordinary shares of twenty-five pence each fully paid in Megastores plc, subject to the memorandum and articles of association of the company.

Issued under the common seal of the company

S-E-A-L

NOTE: No transfer of any of the shares comprised in this certificate will be registered until the certificate has been surrendered to the registrar's office: Megabank plc,

Registrar's Dept, PO Box 111, Thread needle Street, London EC1 2CE.

have lower share prices than their less discriminatory peers, since there is a smaller pool of potential buyers.

The share certificate

The share certificate is issued by the registrar (frequently a major bank) of the company in which you have bought shares. (Note that share certificates will not be issued to investors using the Crest or nominee system of share registration, see page 98 and below.) It takes weeks or months to arrive, and several months should be allowed for the arrival of a share certificate from overseas. The certificate is made out with the number of shares held by the stated owner, and there is always a unique identifying code on the certificate (the certificate number, the allocation number, the transfer number or sometimes all of them). Check that the details are correct.

The share certificate is valuable and should be kept in a safe place, such as a bank. For the same reason, you should make note of, and keep safe, the unique code on the certificate. Store a copy of this code separately from the certificate itself. If you lose the certificate (in the post, through theft or through fire), then it is possible to obtain a replacement by writing to the registrar of the company (so be sure to keep that copy of the registration code). You will be obliged to agree to indemnify the company if the original share certificate is fraudulently used (although a thief would find it very difficult to dispose of without your signature). The registrars may charge a substantial fee (£10-£50) for this service.

Important exceptions are bearer share certificates, rare in the UK but quite common in Continental Europe. Unlike most UK share certificates, bearer certificates can be sold by anyone who has them in his possession.

In this respect, they are as valuable as the equivalent sum in bank notes, and they must be as well protected. An ordinary UK share certificate signed away by the investor can also be regarded as a bearer certificate. Share certificates are normally sent through the post 'at the investor's risk'. Usually first class post suffices, and this is used by most issuing companies and brokers. However, the nervous private investor might prefer to send these documents by registered post instead.

Nominee accounts

Some brokers or fund managers hold your shares in nominee accounts. This means that they hold the original share certificate, but you should still receive a statement confirming that you are the beneficial owner of these shares, ie the one to whom all dividends

COUNTRYWIDE STOCKBROKING LIMITED (Incorporating Country, Town, and Co.)

1-4 Broker Street, Thames Valley, TV1 9SB Telephone: 0123-987654

Branches in: Birmingham, Dundee, Edinburgh, Littlemarch-under-Water, London, Manchester, Swansea

Registered Office: Countrywide House, Hampstead, London NW1 9XX Registered in England No. 1234567 VAT

THE BLUEPRINT TO INTELLIGENT INVESTORS

Registration No. 123 4567 89 Regulated by the Financial Services Authority.

Member of the London Stock Exchange

MR. ANTHONY INVESTOR OF NO FIXED ABODE LONDON AB1 9ZY

Bargain Date and Tax Point Security Client Contract

Ref. Settlement Date

O6FEB0X

+0123456

W12345D

A98766

10FEB0X

WE THANK YOU FOR YOUR INSTRUCTIONS AND HAVE SOLD ON YOUR BEHALF AS AGENTS

NEWSTORES ORD 25P

Time Quantity Price Consideration

13:55 1000 1.64 £1640.00

COMMISSION

V.A.T. EXEMPT

COMPLIANCE CHARGE £1640.00

30.00
NIL

5.00

TOTAL

£1605.00

Subject to the Rules and Regulations of the Stock Exchange including any temporary regulations made by or under the authority of the Council of the Stock Exchange.

E. & O.E. V.A.T. Invoice for services rendered (N) = Not subject to V.A.T. Please retain this document for Capital Gains Tax and V.A.T. purposes.

will be paid. PEPs and ISAs are, without exception, nominee accounts. Shares registered with Crest are held predominantly in nominee accounts.

Nominee accounts reduce the amount of paperwork necessary for the agent, which may help to reduce the costs to the investor. There are proposals that all share dealing will in future be carried out through electronic nominee accounts, to save the use of share certificates altogether. These proposals are not universally popular.

Unit trusts

Unit trusts can be purchased by clipping the form from a newspaper and sending it to the fund managers. Alternatively, any broker can buy units for the normal commission. Unit trusts also represent a form of nominee account. Each 'unit' assigned to the investor comprises a stake in a wide range of companies held by the fund manager.

They may be sold through their fund managers. The prices of each trust are usually quoted at least in the Financial Times and often in other newspapers. Unit trusts may also be sold through your broker. When you buy units in a trust, you pay for more of the forthcoming dividend than you will receive. The managers will make a one-off payment in compensation. This is known as equalisation.

Selling shares

Selling shares through a broker involves virtually the same procedure as buying. You must normally have possession of the shares, perhaps in a nominee account, that you are selling. However, if you are still waiting for the share certificate from your broker, he should permit you to sell the shares without the certificate (but not if another broker is involved). Very few brokers will now permit their private clients to 'sell short', ie, sell shares which they do not own. When the contract note arrives, it will be accompanied by a 'transfer note'. This releases your ownership of the shares. Check the details of both contract and transfer notes are correct, then sign the transfer (not the share certificate), and return the transfer and the share certificate to your broker.

The broker will send you payment within a few days. He will not send payment until he has received the share transfer and share certificate.

If the investor dies while holding a portfolio of shares, then the original broker will normally sell the investments for the executor of the estate once probate has been granted.

Selling investment trust shares can be more complex. Any broker will sell the shares in exchange for the share certificate and the full commission. Some trusts will sell the shares for you at a reduced price, others will give you the name of a broker (not your own broker) who will sell the shares at a reduced commission rate. Yet other trusts will have your share holding, if purchased through a savings scheme, in a nominee account and the shares will have to be released from this before you, or the trust, can sell them.

Renunciation/splitting/consolidation

Temporary share certificates are provided in the first instance for new share issues (eg government privatisations) and rights issues. These are complicated documents filled with legalistic jargon in very small print. Summaries are given on an adjacent page showing the important features.

These temporary certificates are valuable documents and must not be lost. They are used to support changes in ownership before the permanent share certificate is issued, and then have no further value. Details of how to handle the temporary forms vary slightly from case to case, so it is essential to read the document thoroughly. The following provides a typical example. If you sell your temporary certificate, then you are said to have 'renounced' it. Fill in 'Form X' (Form of Renunciation) on the back of the certificate and send the certificate to the stockbroker or other agent. The new purchaser will fill in 'Form Y' (Registration Application Form) to register his new ownership. Several purchased temporary certificates can be registered together (consolidation). The broker, or agent, will fill in 'Form Z'; in the case of a private transaction, without going through a broker, fill in the buyer's name in Form Z. Forms 'X, Y and Z' are traditionally printed on the back of temporary certificates.

If the investor wishes to sell only part of his share holding on the temporary certificate, then he is said to split the certificate. The same forms 'X, Y and Z' are filled in and sent with a covering letter to the company registrar stating how many shares should be sent on to a new purchaser and how many sent back on a temporary certificate to the original investor.

A complication is caused by rights issues. The temporary certificate has a small value of its own even while the purchase price of the shares on it has not been paid and the shares are known as 'nil-paid'. After the payment has been made for the new shares, the temporary certificate will be stamped by the registrar and returned temporarily to the original investor, pending arrival of the definitive certificate. These shares are known as 'fully paid' (or as 'part paid' if payment is to be made in several instalments).

'Splitting' the temporary certificate for rights issues can normally be done on or before two separate dates:

- an early date for 'nil paid' shares
- a later date for 'fully paid' shares.

If the investor declines either to take up his rights issue (ie, purchase the shares he has been allocated) or to sell them nil paid, then many companies issuing the rights shares will attempt to sell the rights nil paid in the open market and will then send the investor any proceeds so obtained, less expenses (normally subject to a minimum).

'Bed-and-breakfast'

'Bed-and-breakfasting' used to mean selling shares and buying them back again on the following working day. This was invariably done for tax reasons, usually to settle the capital gains liability on the day the shares were sold. This tax avoidance scheme was banned in 1998.

Share registers are public documents

The share registers of public companies are, in effect, public documents. Anyone can demand that the company makes its share register available, and the law requires that the register must be provided.

Several marketing agencies have trawled the registers of some of the government's privatisation issues (notoriously those of British Telecom and British Gas), so that anyone who subscribed for shares in these companies is likely to find themselves on numerous junk mail lists. Those investors who are found on several share registers are likely to receive special attention from charities and the sellers of holiday homes, gold-plated pens, luxury yachts and other up¬market paraphernalia. Some companies allow use of their own nominee account to disguise the identity of their shareholders. For example, the pharmaceutical company GlaxoSmithKline.

When To Buy And When To Sell

Don't stay in too long

It is not always necessary or desirable to remain fully invested in the stock market. The ability to match the average performance of the market is of small comfort when the average is falling. If you can predict a market crash, then it will pay you to anticipate it by 'going liquid' - selling out for cash.

Recent experience suggests that index-linked gilts may provide the best home for funds pulled out before a bear market, assuming, of course, that the bear market occurred. This is because in recent years inflation has been a serious worry and the cause of share price underperformance.

However, index-linked gilts would be a poor investment if a depression occurred. Under these circumstances there is no money anywhere and inflation may even be negative.

Index-linked gilts show an increase in capital value (at the repayment date) which is based on the government's official inflation rate, the Retail Prices Index (RPI). Any alteration in the basis of calculation of the RPI permits investors to demand instant repayment. The government has indicated that index- linked gilts would not drop in value if inflation were negative.

Ordinary gilts have proved in recent decades to be a poor investment since their fixed income repayments are reduced in real terms by inflation. They ought to be a good investment in a depression and have indeed performed well in the early 2000s.

The start of a bull market

Bull markets start only a few times during an investor's active career, so it is essential not to miss them. Various warning signs of the start of a bull market are known, for example:

- Short-term interest rates fall.
- The 'yield gap' narrows (page 35).
- There is a sudden fall in the market as everyone agrees that it is not worth hanging on any longer and sells out.
- The Coppock Indicator starts to rise from a negative index.

THE COPPOCK INDICATOR

Historically, one of the most reliable predictors of the start of a bull market has been the Coppock Indicator. This indicator has also been used, less reliably, to predict the start of a bear market.

The Coppock Indicator is loosely based on 'Wave Theory', which says in substance that stock market performance ebbs and flows in cycles (the economic cycle). It follows that the Indicator is only of value for predicting long term changes in investment sentiment, and is useless for predicting sudden surges of enthusiasm or moments of panic like the October 1987 crash. The Indicator may be regarded as a general measure of underlying investor confidence.

The Coppock Indicator is calculated in a complex manner:

1. Take this month's average share price index and subtract the average index for the same month twelve months ago. Multiply the result by ten.
2. Repeat this arithmetic for last month and multiply the result by nine (instead of by ten). Repeat this

sequence for a total of ten months, multiplying each successive result by eight, seven, six and so on down to one.

3. Add up all the figures calculated in steps (1) and (2). The result may be positive or negative. Divide the result by ten. The figure so obtained is the Coppock Indicator for this month.

These laborious calculations are done for you and published monthly by the Investors' Chronicle.

An average indicator value of zero is taken as the base line. If the Coppock value is above zero, a bull market exists, while a figure below zero indicates the existence of a bear market.

The start of a bull market is predicted when the points plotted below zero first start to become less bad. Thus, if the figures for January, February, March and April were -100, -110, -112, and -110, then April would give the first sign of a new bull market. The Coppock Indicator has worked well in the past (and is self- fulfilling if everyone believes it), but has been criticised for being too slow to respond. Therefore, a certain measure of anticipation is needed by the investor. Start to buy shares when the Indicator looks as though it is about to turn and hope that there is no sudden reversal.

The Indicator is particularly slow to respond after a market crash. The Coppock Indicator recommended selling stock in December 1987, just as the market bottomed! It can be a useful tool then, but must be used with caution. In particular, it is only of value if there have been no violent changes in the stock market indices in the preceding twelve months.

The Coppock Indicator last turned up again from a negative value in May 2003.

CHAPTER 4

Is It Possible To Become A Millionaire?

Of course it is possible to become a millionaire. My father told me a saying that a Jewish man told him once. "Even if you shovel dirt for a living as long as you stick to it you will make a million dollars." Obviously knowing how to manage your money is the start of becoming a millionaire. As it has been said "The more you make the more you spend."

First of all this is going to be a no B.S. basic guide to get you make money. But, it isn't going to be easy at first, you will have to put time effort to get is started. Once you get started and see how much money is up to you.

There are 4 types of industries that make money to be a millionaire fast.

1. **Real Estate** - Everyone know the real estate is great for make money. But, a beginners with have difficulty even getting a loan from a bank these days
2. **Stock Market Investing** - Stock market is going to down the tubes these days the only things that are making a profit are stuff that isn't good for

everyone. Like cigarette, oil, energy companies, etc. You get the point.

3. **Business** - Its great having your own business but again you will need capital. First your going have to pay to lease a place/building, pay employees, buy product at whole sale then sale it at retail cost. Not to forget shipping costs. This type work will take your whole day away from you.

4. **Internet Business** - This the best and easy way even the quickest way. Just a small investment in a domain name. You can sell information which doesn't cost you in shipping. No employees to pay. You keep all the profit except the 3% the credit cards take when someone purchase with a credit card.

The time put into start an internet business is the set up. But once setup, the only time need is in advertising and even ways for free. There many ways to advertise online. There is Google AdWords, Craigslist, post banners, new groups, and more. First start up a website with something you enjoy doing, such as a hobby or pleasure of yours.

Simple Truth Can Help You Become a Millionaire

The old adage that "the truth will set you free" is still as applicable today as it was eons of ages ago when this simple grain of wisdom was taught by a renowned leader of that era. If indeed truth literally can set me free, then it means that it can give me freedom from all of my wants and give me abundance. If truth is indeed as powerful as this, then discovering truths can help me become a millionaire. This conjecture leads to a lot of questions such as:

What are the simple truths about millionaires?

Where can I find the simple truths that will help me become a millionaire?

How can I use the simple truth to help me become a millionaire?

These actually are the simple questions asked about the simple truth that can help me become a millionaire. So the secret really is to know the right answers to these simple questions.

What are the simple truths about millionaires?

It is the very simple truth that anyone determined enough can improve his lot in life. Aside from determination, of course, is the willingness to live out the truths that can help one really become a millionaire. It's evident that anyone can accumulate wealth, if they are disciplined enough, determined to persevere, and have the merest of luck. The following are the simple truths about millionaires that you can follow as a guide for yourself in the pursuit of wealth:

1. Millionaires live a very simple life.
2. Millionaires allocate funds efficiently in ways that build wealth, and they avoid conspicuous consumption.

3. Millionaires are proficient in targeting marketing opportunities.
4. Millionaires are proficient in choosing the right occupation.
5. Millionaires are mostly self-employed, in other words, most of them are entrepreneurs.

The traits above are the general characteristics or traits of millionaires. If you live your life in accordance with these simple truths about millionaires, living a simple life, living below your means, and grabbing opportunities as they come, then you are well on your way and are ready to digest the other set of truths that can help you become a millionaire.

Where can I find the truth that can help me become a millionaire?

We have already delved on the simple truths about millionaires, but there are still other truths to find. We need not look far and wide to know our way to becoming a millionaire. The simple truth is that in our day and age, the means to becoming wealthy are just around the corner. For example, the net is full of opportunities to earn an income. You just have to develop your skills at detecting an earning opportunity that you can find in the net.

You may ask, how does this truth about income opportunities in the internet ever help me accumulate wealth and help me become a millionaire? Very simple. You just have to grab all the opportunities that you can, and of course as you grab it, so you earn money. Now is that enough to make you wealthy? The answer is no! You have to stick by those simple truths above concerning millionaires if you ever are to become a millionaire yourself. That is, never spend what you earn as soon as you earn it. Live way below what you make. That is how millionaires live. Follow their cue and you can become one of them yourself.

A simple reminder, no matter how much you want to become a millionaire, without hardwork, patience, self motivation and confidence reaching your dreams of becoming a millionaire is far from reality.

Become a Millionaire Investing - The Secret to Making Millions With Little Or No Risk!

Once you make the decision to become a millionaire investing, the next thing is working out your investment strategy. Whilst choosing the right professional and career path can help earn a greater income, it's what you do with your earned income that counts. You can't earn your way to wealth. You've gotta invest your earned income, turning it into passive or portfolio income so that your money works for you.

Risk = Not Knowing What You're Doing

In business, life and investing, you have to decide not whether to take risk, but rather, what kind of risk(s) to take. Every investment or business decision implies some element of risk ranging from low to high.

The Cambridge dictionary refers to risk as 'the possibility of something bad happening'. When it comes to investing money, many people think of risk as the possibility of losing part or all of their money. Investment professionals can refer to risk as the 'variability of returns' and your typical fund manager will see risk as the difference between expectation and results. My all-time favourite quote about risk comes from none other than Warren Buffet: "Risk comes from not knowing what you're doing". I think this nails it.

The Investor...The Biggest Risk in Investing?

The biggest risk with investing is not so much the investment vehicle but actually the investor. If an investor can plan, remain unemotional and become financial literate than riches and wealth are guaranteed.

Many financial advisors and professionals speak of understanding risk and the inherent trade-off between risk and reward. But oftentimes, this falls on deaf ears and people ignore the risk associated with their investment strategies. Why is this?

Well, there are 3 likely reasons

1. Many Investors Don't Have a Plan

A plan can simply entail having objectives and timeframes. Planning for retirement in 20 or 30 years time requires a different investment strategy than planning for your children's education or investing in a home in 3 to 5 years time. When you have a plan you are less likely to go off-plan and follow your friends and family into the latest hot-tip investment. You are less likely to get sold on some high-risk, speculative foreign property investment for example. Once you are clear on your objectives and timeframes, and don't let your emotions get in the way (see reason no.2) then you can become rich and build wealth assuredly.

2.   Many Investors Invest Emotionally

Many investments are made foolishly because it makes the investor feel good in the short-term. Buying gold coins, a 5-bedroom villa or a plot of land may make us feel good about ourselves and gives us bragging-rights when we're out and about socially buy oftentimes (not always) these are speculative, high-risk, income sucking money pits. Investing is an intellectual sport.

Irrational exuberance has no place on the playing field. Time, patience and discipline are your best friends, impulse your enemy. It never ceases to amaze me how hard people work for their money and then drop money into some glossy, so-called investment product so easily. Investing is a plan, not a product. Asking yourself the question "What Don't I See" or "What Could Go Wrong Here" are vital questions to answer before signing on the dotted line of any investment.

3.   Many Investors are Not Financially Literate

Many investors are over-reliant on their financial advisors, accountants and conjecture. The best reason to become financially literate is not so you can control all your investments but rather that you know what questions to ask your financial advisors and then fully understand their answers. Understanding the costs of an investment (management fees, commissions, taxes) is so unbelievably important. Reducing these costs to a minimum will have a massive effect on your portfolio's value and your wealth. For example, if the investment return is 10% before costs, and intermediation costs are approximately 2%, then you earn 8%. Compounded over 50 years, 8% turns $10,000 into $469,000. But if you could reduce those intermediary costs to 0%, you earn 10%, and the final value is a staggeringly different value of $1,170,000 - nearly three times as much!

Become Your Own Financial Advisor

Investing itself is not risky; not being financially literate is. The key to risk reduction is improved investor 'financial literacy' and reducing over-reliance on accountants, financial advisors and so on. You have to become your own financial advisor. Paying close attention to the seemingly innocuous 1.5 or 2% management/commission fees is vital. As you can see from the above example, they are an insidious eroder of wealth and need to be negotiated down, avoided and minimised where possible. Having an imperfect plan of some kind with objectives and timeframes is truly better than having no plan at all.

Finally, becoming financially literate should become your mission in life if you are to reduce risk and increase the certainty and velocity of return so that you become rich with certainty and make those millions you've dreamed off.

The Millionaire Mindset - How to Have the Millionaire Mindset and Become Wealthy Fast

What is the millionaire mindset? Who can have it? How can you have it? Before I answer those questions, let me tell you something about millionaires in general.

Most millionaires aren't really afraid of anything. Sometimes, even against their advisers, they make a decision and end up being all the better for it. Most millionaires also tend to have an amazing amount of energy whether it's directed at their work or at their peers.

Now that you know it, doesn't it seem fun to become a millionaire? I'm not just talking about acquiring millions of dollars here. That comes later. The first and most important requirement is to have the millionaire mindset.

Aggressiveness in Business

Aggressiveness is part of the millionaire mindset. After all, you're not going to get anywhere unless you pursue something in a big way.

For example, you want to earn millions by setting up your own coffee shop. But if you stay meek and quiet in your little corner, how could you expect to compete with the more established brands just across the street from you?

You have to turn on your aggressive switch, start advertising and marketing your product. Make some noise and you'll make yourself some money.

Love for Craft

Having the millionaire mindset does not mean you have to work hard at a job you hate. That's not how it works.

Most millionaires earn the big bucks when they genuinely love what they do. Find your interest and work that angle. This way, you won't get tired of it soon; and you'll be many times more eager to pursue it.

If working on a certain job or project has a high earning potential but you end up being unhappy, it's just not worth it. You'll probably quit one day before you even achieve anything worthwhile.

Relentless Positivity

Millionaires don't waste their time worrying that something might go wrong, or that a screw is going to loosen. Instead, they direct all their energies into attracting abundance and success in their business.

Having a positive mindset is having the millionaire mindset. Think of yourself as a fortunate person; luck and wealth will soon find their way to you.

Having the millionaire mindset will help make every day of your life richer, fuller and altogether more satisfying. You may not be a millionaire now; but once you adopt the millionaire mindset, you'll be as good as one!

How An Average Person Can Become A Millionaire - Step By Step Directions

Millionaires are definitely in the minority & this is absolutely no accident. The main reason why most people aren't wealthy is because most people simply do not want to be rich. If you asked most of the people that you know if they would like to make a million they most likely would say yes. The thing is that most people wouldn't mind receiving a million dollars if they didn't have to do anything out of their way to receive it. Many people do not make money their first priority.

If you asked the masses to name their top 5 priorities in life, they would generally prioritize them in the following order:

1. Family
2. Living Expenses
3. Entertainment
4. Vacations
5. Retirement

Now here are a Millionaire's Priorities:

1. Family
2. Making More Money
3. Focus
4. Opportunity
5. Constant Growth

Do you see the difference in the mindset above? The first group seems to focus on survival & entertainment.

The second group seems to focus on prosperity. Think about this for one minute. If you focus on just paying bills & surviving then that is what you will be doing for a very long time.

Now if you changed your focus to making more money instead of just paying off debts, then entertainment, vacations, retirement & living expenses will be the by product of making more income.

Here is the main problem: Most people do not want to take any more time than they have to put in at their jobs to earn income. After work they rush home to spend what little time they have left in the day to be with their families or to do something they enjoy.

Here are some more comparisons in the mind set of the masses to the millionaire:

Millionaires focus on getting paid for their efforts. The masses focus on getting paid for their time.

Millionaires don't mind working 7 days per week or after hours if they have to. The masses only want to work during business hours.

Millionaires don't think a road block is a problem. They just look at it as something that needs a solution. The masses will tend to become petrified at the first road block.

If you truly want to become wealthy then you have got to start thinking like a millionaire right now even if you don't have the money yet.

Many Millionaires were not born rich. Many came from poverty.

Anyone can become a millionaire by using the following 5 steps:

1. Seek Wisdom
2. Income Goal
3. Timing
4. Opportunity
5. Commitment

Seek Wisdom:

Start building your mind everyday by educating yourself personally. Read books & go to seminars on wealth building. Surround yourself with like minded individuals.

Model rich & famous people. Seek out a mentor. Make a decision to change your mindset as of today.

Millionaires are constantly building their minds & getting coached. They know that no matter how much they have accomplished, there is always room for growth.

Income Goal:

I will guess that your goal is a million dollars if you are reading this article but is that believable to you? Here is an example of what I mean: If someone only made $50,000 per year but wanted to make a million instead then that would be making 20 times more than what they are used to. It is a very big stretch. It would be easier to make an income goal of $80,000 instead. $80,000 is more believable for someone who only makes $50K.

Now once they achieve $80K, then they can change their income goal to $100K & so on. Pick an income goal & write it down.

Timing:

Find out when you want to start making this kind of income. Don't wait for the opportunity to present itself. Instead give yourself a realistic deadline. If you say something like "sometime this year" then you have absolutely no idea & may never get started on your road to abundance. Pick a date for example: I want to increase my income by $30K by the next 6 months. Pick a date & write it down.

Opportunity:

Now once you have a date & time then you can start looking for opportunities to increase your immediate cash flow. Look for a second source of income that can give you a residual income stream. Residual income will give you extra income without the constant extra effort. It is always better to keep doing what you are currently doing for your primary income while at the same time building a second income stream. Once you have a second income stream bringing you a constant flow of income, find another opportunity & repeat.

This is where it gets tricky. Most people try to build 3 or 4 multiple income streams at the same time but do not experience success in any of them because they get overwhelmed. Start with one opportunity at a time.

Commitment:

Make a commitment to yourself that you will do everything humanly possible to get what you want as long as you do not hurt anyone. Stick with your plans no matter how many road blocks you hit. In order to earn a million dollars (which is out of the ordinary) you will have to take the road less travelled. Stick to your guns & you will achieve your desired outcome. This is what makes a millionaire a millionaire. Their desire is so strong that they stay in the game long enough to reap their rewards.

Discover the Holy Grail Which Helps You to Become a Millionaire

Becoming a millionaire doesn't happen all at once. Of course, it entails some serious toils, dedication, hard work and tons of discipline. You cannot also become a millionaire overnight in just a snap of your fingers. For years, entrepreneurs keep searching for the Holy Grail which they think would help them become a millionaire. The truth of the matter is that there could be no thing as such. Instead, they could learn some straightforward life disciplines that would help them become a millionaire. Here are some nifty ways that would be valuable in helping you become a millionaire. True enough these may sound easy not until you start applying it to the way you deal with your finances.

Learn How to Save

What do you automatically do right after receiving your paycheck? Some people seemed clueless on how to handle their finances. The instance they receive their pay, the very first thing that shoots up their mind could be shopping. Millionaires do not think this way. Instead, they allocate a portion of their incomes for savings before spending it. Their equation is that income minus savings is equal to their expenses. There's also a rule that would help you become a millionaire and it's called the Pareto Principle of 80/20. This means that you have to set a meager 20 per cent of your income as your savings and the remaining 80 per cent will be spent for your miscellaneous expenses. The bottom line is that you should learn how to make both ends meet with the remaining 80 per cent. That's how financial dealings should be.

Live Within or Below Your Means

Paradoxically speaking, true millionaires do not live an affluent kind of style. However, we may be too convinced with how the media describes the life of a millionaire which includes living in a mansion, driving expensive cars and relishing other lavish means of living. The truth of the matter is that these millionaires actually live a simple kind of life. They don't wear designer clothes nor drive expensive cars but when you check their bank accounts, you would be surprised to find out their huge wealth.

Value Time

Time is essential for millionaires. They keep track of their time and they start young. They also make use of the time to hone their skills in dealing with their finances.

Different Sources of Income

Also, millionaires do not just rely in one income source. They do not just put forth their investments in one venture. This is to ensure that in any case that one source of income would come to its demise; they would still have another income streaming from another source.

Set Your Goals

Most importantly, millionaires set their smart goals. This would serve as a peg for their actions. It is indeed a rough road on the pursuit to become a millionaire. There can be a lot of tough times and uncertainties. However, with these goals and the right determination, becoming a millionaire is never too elusive.

Indeed, there's no such thing as the Holy Grail to become a millionaire. Rather, there are disciplines and principles which would help propel you to become a millionaire. Act now and you're sure to reap the benefits sooner than you expected.

Become A Millionaire - 9 Must Have Entrepreneurial Qualities To Create Millionaire Wealth

Let me help you realize your dreams to become a millionaire and experience financial freedom.

In this article I aim to share with you some entrepreneurial qualities that will help turbo-charge your wealth and success.

1,400 Self-Made Millionaires are made everyday?

In 2005 Forbes Magazine revealed these amazing facts:

There were 691 reported billionaires in the world.

And 1,400 individuals became millionaires' everyday.

Do you want to be one of them?

I have no doubt you do!

You aspire, just like everybody else to be independently wealthy. To be free to do the business in the way you want.

To be free from irritating bosses and close-minded supervisors.

So much power is felt and done in running your own business enterprise and there is nothing like having a business that runs itself!

This is the ultimate goal of aspiring entrepreneurs. Unless you win the lottery it is unlikely you'll become a millionaire overnight but you can achieve it in a relatively short space of time if you follow the steps of the rich and successful.

As Anthony Robbins says, "Success leaves clues"

The Quest For Freedom

Dreaming and aspiring for wealth is not only about having money, it's also about having more freedom.

Freedom from debt-freedom from want-freedom to choose the future for your children.

Do you want your kids to go to school that they want to? Do you want to be free from debt?

Of Course!

Now the next critical question is how can you be free? How can we be one of the 1,400 who become self-made millionaires everyday?

Let me share with you some characteristics that self-made millionaires have in common.

One commonality that can be seen is that there is a large number of self-made millionaires that have made their wealth online.

But these characteristics are not only common amongst online millionaires but in all self-made millionaires.

So here we go

1.   Self-Made Millionaires Do Not Blame-

They are never party to the blame culture.

When a mistake is made they do not look for who made the mistake but they look for ways in how to fix the mistake.

No excuses are made for bad outcomes or portion the blame to someone else. Successful business persons learn from their mistakes and very rarely repeat them.

2.   Millionaires are Decisive and They Have a Vision of What They Want To Do and Happen-

They strive and push towards their visions and goals.

To achieve your millionaire goal you must have a target and the drive to seek the means to achieve your targets.

3.   Millionaires follow and trust their intuition -

Millionaires follow their nose. If they believe that an idea or a concept will work then pursue it, if it does not feel right then they abandon the idea.

4.   Millionaires are Focused on Their Core Expertise and Core Business-

The successful business persons follow their main line of expertise. Yes they do snatch up a good idea when they see it - but they stay focused on their primary vision.

Yes it is true that they are doing a lot of tasks- e.g. Online marketer- marketing on Ebay, writing articles, attending training seminars and digesting more knowledge but all of these sum up to their main goals

5.   Millionaires are Focused on Marketing-

You must look at the success of one of the richest individual in the planet-Steve Jobs of Apple.

He focuses on his core business; he hires and recognizes the need for and the importance of marketing.

You must focus on marketing to gain exposure and constantly look to expanding your audience. --- write emails, do online and offline advertising, press releases etc.

Simply put if you want a fair income that pays the bills-then you market and sell products and services.

But if you want to be crazy rich then you must create and control markets and market demands.

Thus the key to eye-popping business success is strategic marketing.

6.   You Have to Understand the Need for Continuing Your Education- Education is not just confined to the four walls of a classroom. You can learn from many people, from their life's experiences even from their perceptions.

You have to listen-sincerely listen to others, how they achieved their success and how they also got their failures.

-- Also how they overcame those failures.

Go to training seminars, learn from the web, E-books, videos blogs everything.

You have to look at these new strategies and see how they can help you in your business and achieve your goals.

7.   Do Not Be Afraid of Making Mistakes- Any big success, any company, any individual has had their own share of failures.

Thomas Edison is a perfect example of someone learning from his 'failures' and never giving up. The story has it that it took him over 10,000 attempts to invent the light bulb, and he responded saying, "I have not failed. I've just found 10,000 ways that won't work".

The huge online companies like eBay and Craigslist have had its own share of failures. What distinguishes them from the complete failures is simply this:

You have to learn from your mistakes, rise to the occasion, persevere and persist.

Nobody said it was ever going to be easy.

8.   You Have to Model Your Business for Success- You have to look for successful business models and paradigms to pattern after. Internet-based enterprises do this all the time.

You have to learn about the competition. You have to learn how there systems work for you.

Some have this as "Reverse Engineering" but I would prefer to call it aggressive research. - Get their products and learn how they achieve success.

9.   You Have to Build a Team That You Can Trust- Two heads are better than one-I learned this the hard way. No matter how good you think you are you must rely on the inputs and outputs of a trusted team.

A great team of like-minded individuals is not difficult to find. You can find them on seminars and any public forums.

Making a fortune - getting wealth is a team endeavor.

Just look at the many teams that have achieved greatness-modern history is rife with them.

Now that you have learned of the 9 characteristics that you need to have-then you can start putting things in place so that you develop the mindset and actions of millionaires.

To increase your chances of success try to make sure you adhere to the 9 characteristics to become a millionaire. Use what you've learned and be patient!! These things do not happen overnight - Rome wasn't built in a day— but that empire lasted for thousands of years!

To Become a Millionaire, You Must Learn to Act Like One

In order to learn to act like a millionaire there are two simple concepts that you need to come to understand and implement. When these two concepts are implemented in your life you will be well on your way to financial freedom and success.

The first concept you need to understand is the T-F- A=R equation. This is the equation that explains where all results ultimately come from. What this equation means is that our thoughts become our feelings which become our actions which equal our results. When we act like a millionaire me get the result of becoming a millionaire.

But prior to acting like a millionaire we must first start thinking and feeling like one so we can learn to act like one. The key to any success is learning to think like the person you desire to become. Millionaires do think differently than non-millionaires. They see every dollar as something they can use to grow more money, they find opportunities, they see every person as a possible collaborator and/or client, etc. Thinking about money, people and success differently changes how they feel.

As they think differently they start to change their feeling to be more in alignment with their goals. Instead of feeling like all rich people are greedy, they start to feel like they can help more people the more money they have.. It is not just feelings towards others that change it is also how you will feel about yourself. You will have more confidence in your ability to become a millionaire, you will know in your gut, feel that it is a reality for you.

Once that shift has occurred that leads you to feeling like you are a millionaire then you will start to take all of the actions you need in order to become a millionaire. Once you take those actions then you will start to see the results coming your way to match it.

And the second concept you need to learn is a concept you can start implementing right now to help make that shift towards acting like a millionaire a reality even if the thoughts and feelings have not caught up yet. This concept will help you to start acting like a millionaire, even in a little way, starting immediately.

The way to start acting like a millionaire is to start acting like one. Take 10% of your income and put it aside to act like a millionaire every month. Depending on how much this will decide what you do. You could fly first class on your next flight, or you could take a limo to the airport. Maybe go to a restaurant and order the fish at Market Price without asking how much market price is. Buy the bottle of wine recommended by the waiter. Do one thing you would usually not do because you usually think 'I can't afford it".

If you put into effect the T-F-A=R equation and start using your play money to act like a millionaire one a month you will be on your way to success. If you think, feel and act like a millionaire you are moving positively towards becoming one.

How Do I Become a Millionaire - Reduce Taxes and Manage Cash Flow

An important "how do I become a millionaire" step is to reduce taxes legally. Taxes are the highest expense of the working middle class. However, the government does give you tax breaks if you own your own business.

Now I'm not saying to start a frivolous business to get tax breaks... that would be illegal. But, you can start a legitimate business with the intent to make money and get tax breaks by doing so.

One way this works is that with a business, you get to deduct your expenses from your income and then only pay on the remaining balance. With the working middle class, you have to pay taxes and then your income covers your additional expenses. That is a huge difference!

How do I become a millionaire if I'm being taxed at the highest rate possible? The answer is that it is very difficult.

So.... what kind of business can you start? You can do an online internet business, a multi-level marketing business, or anything that you have a passion about. The more passionate you are about it, the more successful you'll be.

Passion drives us to new heights so focus your passion into a business.

Seek wise counsel, start your own business, and receive some amazing tax reductions. You'll be amazed at where this can take you!

Managing your cash flow is another important step towards your financial freedom. How can I become a millionaire by managing cash flow, and what is that anyway? Cash flow is the amount of money coming in to you and going out from you. Money is always moving.

However, if you are using all the money coming in to you to cover expenses you have no extra cash. You will always be wondering if you are going to have too much month at the end of your paycheck. This is true if you are earning $20,000, $40,000, $100,000 or even $1,000,000.

If you always spend everything you make, you'll always be broke. You may have more toys when you earn more, but you'll still be broke. So another "how do I become a millionaire" step is creating a strategy to manage cash flow. A common strategy used by rich people is to give 10% of their income away, save 10%, and invest 10%, and spend what's left on expenses and buying things they enjoy.

If the percentages are too high for you right now, then use a smaller percentage. However, if you are going to become a millionaire, start doing the things that millionaires do even if it is on a smaller scale. Then set a goal to get to right percentages and categories for you, but do not spend everything you make.

These are just two simple steps that can make a profound difference in where you end up, financially. When you take action on this advice, you've just taken two more steps towards a brighter future. You'll feel good about mastering your cash flow, and you can take pride in managing your own business.

SAMPLE Step by Step Blueprint to Become a Millionaire

Strategy: First sale (Grind Stage)

If you have written an article, set-up a PPC campaign, made a forum post, recommended a friend, or otherwise, you have taken your first step towards making your first sale. The first sale could come in a variety of ways, but once you make this sale, things will become real very quickly.

The first sale is always the toughest within any industry. Once you make one sale, it is pretty easy to make ten. Once you make 10, it is easy to make 100 (and so on). So the first sell is where you have to grind it out.

Implement one of the steps from the guide, whether it be article marketing or PPC, and start building your campaigns. The more articles you have out there promoting your product, the greater the chance you are going to make your first sale. Same with PPC...the more ad groups that you have running, the greater the chance!

The absolute worst thing you can do is quit! Quitters never get ahead. Learn from your mistakes and continue building and taking action. Action leads to winning campaigns.

Strategy: $100/day (Building Stage)

Alright, you have made your first sale. SWEET!

Now is time to kick things into high gear. At this point the opportunity is real. You can see green and you can see the potential to make a lot more money, the first goal being your first $i00/day.

If you break this down, $100/day would require you to make 2.6 sales per day. This should not be too difficult.

What does it take to achieve this? A work schedule! It will take some work to achieve this, but it will not take too much. A single ad group or a single article could earn you 2.6 sales per day no problem, so now is time to build your campaigns up.

Here are the tasks you should set for yourself (choose one):

Article Marketing - 2 articles/day (focusing on different keywords), submit and social bookmark

Pay-Per-Click - build 2 landing pages per day targeting different keywords and then create 2 corresponding ad groups within Google AdWords or Yahoo Search Marketing.

Forums / Q & A Sites - make 20 posts/comments per day, promoting a product in your signature or within the actual post.

The key is to start building at this point. The more you build, the better you are setting yourself up for the next step, the $1000/day. It is important that once you earn a bit of money that you don't go off and buy yourself a new TV.

Put the money you earn straight back into your business. Buy more PPC traffic or start outsourcing your article writing. Now is the time to build, later is the time to start spending (once you earn enough that a new TV won't make even a little dent in your budget!).

Strategy: $1,000/day (Fully Leveraged Stage)

Boom, you have hit a consistent $i00/day mark. It is time to take your business to the next level.

You are essentially earning a good level of seed money that can now be used to take your business to the next level.

All of your profits at this point should be put directly back into your business. It is now time to start growing and leveraging your income to build your campaigns and pages more quickly and efficiently.

Broken down, $i000/day is 25.7 sales per day. This is not a lot when you think of the scope of the industry, especially when top affiliates in this industry make 100+ sales per day.

You need to continue building (choose one):

Article Marketing - 2 articles/day (focusing on different keywords), submit and social bookmark

Pay-Per-Click - build 2 landing pages per day targeting different keywords and then create 2 corresponding ad groups within Google AdWords or Yahoo Search Marketing.

If you are using strictly article marketing at this point, you need to start using PPC as well. You can easily port over existing (and successful) article campaigns into paid ones and often times double your earnings overnight, so some of your earnings need to be put into PPC at this point.

$1000/day is not going to happen overnight, but is definitely realistic if you continue building your campaign for the next 6 months.

If you build 2 pages per day for 6 months, you are going to have 360 pages and ad groups out there receive traffic. Let's say you can get just 5 clicks/day to each page.

360 pages * 5 clicks = 1800 clicks

If you convert at 1:50 (top affiliates convert at 1:20), you will make 36 sales every day, which would exceed the $1000/day mark ($1396.44 to be exact).

$1000/day is definitely possible for YOU! Anyone can achieve this goal if the build based on the blueprint provided here, but the main thing is growing your business organically...meaning any money you earn, you put back into your business. This allows you to grow much quicker and expand your overall earnings much quicker.

In the final strategy, we are going to show you how you can become a millionaire SUPER AFFILIATE!

Strategy: $1,000,000/year (High Octane Stage)

Alright, things are going really good now. You are at the $1000/day level, pulling in around $30K every month. This all started with a single sale and looking back you could do it again if you wanted to.

To earn $1,000,000 per year, you need to make $2,739.73/day. This is equivalent to 70.6 product referrals per day.

This may seem like a lot, but if you have reached this point already, all you need to do is pretty much double your existing business. As mentioned, top affiliates make well over 100+ sales per day, so this is a reality. This is something that YOU can achieve.

You have a sizeable budget to grow and expand your business at this point. You can outsource a lot of your content development, start incorporating email marketing campaigns into the mix (collect visitor

emails and back-end a site), and you can continue building your campaigns as usual.

If you continue for the next 6 months building just 2 pages per day, you will have 720 pages getting traffic. If each get 5 clicks/day, that will be over 3600 people coming to your website every day.

If 3600 people convert at 1:50, you will make 72 sales per day which will take you over the million dollar mark! You will be a mill-ion-freakin-aire! This is the dream.

A turn-key business that will make you this sort of loot regardless of whether you are there or not and has room to still expand! Once you have this sort of budget you can get people to do the things for you that you don't want to do.

1. Outsource 100 articles promoting your product...get you a crap load more traffic!
2. Outsource the development of 5 websites, then outsource the content development of those sites incorporating your product reviews and promotions!
3. Seek out ad positioning on related sites...sometimes you can find great deals and triple or quadruple the money you spent for advertising overnight!
4. Get bonuses developed that you give away to anyone that purchases your product on/through your site

The ideas to leveraging your situation become massive and $1MM per year become a quick reality. This should be your goal and we hope you can now realize the potential promoting a product through Internet. The system works, it converts, and it is helping people to solve their problem. This is something that you can be confident promoting as you know it will truly help people achieve their goals.

How To Apply The Law Of Attraction To Become A Millionaire

What exciting times we live in! Since The secret came out so many more people are now "wakened" to the idea of being able to direct their destiny! I have come across a lot of people wanting to apply the Law of Attraction, particularly to attract more wealth and fortune into their lives. It is probably one of the most important areas for which people truly see a change to transform their reality. At the same time I have read numerous books and articles devoting at least one chapter to this topic. In this article I thought I'd share some of the techniques I came across and techniques I use myself.

The first recommended technique is to really see yourself as a millionaire and feel yourself already being a millionaire. Focus on wearing clothes that make you feel prosperous and doing the things a millionaire does, such as looking at amazing houses and going out for lunch. Really focus on wealth and abundance instead of on lack or limitations, not having enough etc as that is what you will keep getting otherwise. If you think you "need" money, that is exactly what you will be attracting to your life: more "needing"! If you feel broke, guess what... you will attract more "brokeness" to your reality.

On the other hand, if you focus on an abundance of money flowing into your life and you really feel this abundance in every fiber of your body, you will create "money attracting vibes"! The interesting thing is, that the more you focus on abundance in your life, the more the "standard" in your mind shifts towards having money. Combined with the right action you will eventually attract that wealth into your reality. Your ideas and feelings shift from "I don't have money" to "I am receiving more and more money" to eventually actually having it.

Another technique is to visualize your actual fortune. If your goal is to become a millionaire, then write out a a check made out to you for 1 million dollars and hang it somewhere in your house where you will see it often. Better still, make copies and hang them all around your house! Visualize a stream of money flowing into your life, like a river. Or visualize your bank account with a million dollars in it. You could even print out a bank statement, white out the amount and replace it with a huge number. See yourself with a full wallet, happily paying diner for a group of friends. Or anything else that you wish you could do if you had the money. Becoming a millionaire is great, but I assume you have this goal because you have some ideas as to how to spend it once earned. So really see yourself already wealthy! What you see in your imagination, is what you will eventually see for real with your eyes! This method is called "vivid visualization" and is extremely powerful. By practicing it, you will find that your self¬image begins to conform to these new images in your mind. You are literally growing into the new successful person you intent to become.

A key factor here is to stop worrying about HOW it will come to you. The universe will take care of that, you need to believe that and focus on positive feelings and vibrations. This will attract the events, circumstances and people into your life to make your goal a reality. Look at your million dollar check and feel the feelings of having that money right now. How would you spend it? How would it feel to spend that kind of money?

A final important point to know, is that if you don't have enough money right now, it means you are blocking the flow of money into your life, with your thoughts. Your wallet speaks very clearly about the vibrations you are sending out into the universe about money at this present moment. So have a really good look at your own beliefs about money. If your beliefs are limiting and scarce, you will need to address this before you can attract your true fortune. You can work on a more positive and abundant belief system by using affirmations. Use affirmations like "I am so happy and excited that I am now attracting a flow of money into my life" or "I easily attract money like a magnet".

Combine the vivid visualization technique with empowering affirmations and the action steps you need to further your goals. This creates a powerful process, and gets you on your way to becoming a millionaire!

Seven Steps You Need to Take to Master Wealth Creation and Become a Millionaire

Millionaire income level is developed all the same way. To become a millionaire, and develop a mastering of wealth creation strategy is fundamentally based on the same seven steps. Every day I start out reviewing my goals and plan to develop financial security. Even during these troubled economic conditions there are ways of mastering wealth creation. You just need to be prepared for the opportunities to generate wealth when they present themselves. Here are seven steps to mastering wealth creation and become a millionaire.

1. Get your act together. Decide that you are going to change the way things are today and change them. You have to make a decision that you want to become wealthy first to become wealthy, this is a mind-set. Eliminate all the negativity that surrounds you and get your act together. Don't let the

distractions of life continue to force you off course. Set your goals and act on them.

2. Get yourself focused on the prize you wish to achieve. No matter what your goals are stay focused. Sure there may be obstacles along the way, and sure you may have challenges to overcome along the way, stay focused! Nothing else should matter but putting in motion a specific plan to achieve your goals that you set up as the ultimate reward and satisfaction of mastering wealth creation. Everything you do in the course of your day should be action toward achieving your goals. If you really want to create a million dollar income and become a millionaire, you are your own worst enemy and without the focus and commitment, to your goal you will not succeed.

3. Get control of your finances. Nothing could be more important than this step, no matter where you are in your plan to create more wealth, you need to evaluate your current financial situation, begin to reduce any frivolous debt, control outgoing expenditures, and regain control of your finances. Yes the old saying is true today as it was in days past, "it takes money to make money." get control of your finances, establish an operating budget, stick to it everyday, freeing up the necessary capital to put forth to build a lucrative cash generating business.

4. Develop a 'positive mental attitude'. Stop for a minute and think, have you ever met a wealthy person that was just miserable because they were wealthy. NO! Most successful people have a great positive mental attitude towards life, and usually

share this with others in their acts of kindness and generosity towards there fellow man. Stop reading the crap in the newspapers and on the internet about how bad things are. Stop watching the news, or listening to others about how tough things are right now. Get into reading books and articles about how to improve your self, be happy and positive and you will attack your plan to mastering wealth creation with more vigor and energy than ever before.

5. Have faith in yourself. Everyone is born with the same skill sets and opportunities to succeed right from birth. Tap into these reserves and stop doubting that you are not as worthy or as deserving as any man that created wealth on this planet has ever been. Most people trudge through life thinking that they were dealt a bad hand, or just don't have what it takes. If your knocked down, Get up! Dust yourself off, and get to work. Have faith that you can master anything you put your mind to, you just have to have the faith in yourself to do so!

6. Browse the money "vehicles" If you already know what yours is, so much the better. You're ready to move forward. if not, do some due diligence to make a sound choice to move forward in your quest to become wealthy. Your money vehicle should be something you can be passionate about, something you can obsess over every waking minute of every day. This "vehicle" should be a driving force that excites you and drives you. This will be the business that will provide the wealth for you as you strive to build it to a multi-million dollar brand.

7. Begin your practical education and training. Once you've selected your path for achieving wealth plug into the training and education needed to develop the expertise to be able to master wealth creation. Access any mode of educating yourself to consume the information to create wealth in the field you have chosen. Find mentors that have gone before you, attend classes and webinars, take positions in relevant arenas to grasp first hand knowledge. Learn as much information necessary to gain confidence in your plan of action to succeed! Review everything you learn from all the courses and systems, choose one, apply it, and commit yourself to just doing it no matter what!

How to Become a Millionaire Fast in Today's Economy - 6 Tips

The majority of today's millionaires are a different breed from those of previous generations, primarily because they have learned how to become a millionaire fast rather than simply inheriting enormous wealth. In 2010 the United States boasted more than 8.4 million households with assets over $1 million, up 8% from the 2009 figures. This figure was still lower than the 2007 high of 9.2 millionaires due to the drop on real estate values, but the steady increase proves you can make your own million even in a struggling economy if you know what you are doing and commit to that. The increasingly numbers of younger entrepreneurs is proof that your first million can be made faster than you might have ever thought possible.

Studying the success stories of these one-generation millionaires shows that they share several common characteristics and strategies that have led them to become financially wealthy and independent. They do not necessarily have the highest IQ, the most important family or political ties or even the most elite education. What they do possess is a drive to succeed at something they are passionate about. This drive pushes them toward their vision with enthusiasm and a positive attitude that draws in the useful support of those around them.

They know both their own strengths and weaknesses and tend to surround themselves with a team that can help them achieve their goals. They are willing to work as long and as hard as it takes because they truly love what they are doing. For example, Mark Zuckerberg, Facebook founder and owner, just recently rented a larger but unexceptional home to be closer to his company offices where he already often works more than 16 hours a day.

The following steps can help you to achieve your financial goals using the same successful strategies millionaires such as Zuckerberg have discovered:

1. Know your own worth. What are you good at and what are you passionate about? What would you love doing all day even if the pay was less than you deserved? The average millionaire makes 17 failed attempts before finding the niche that really works for him/her.
2. Know what you want. Do you want to know the best way to become a millionaire fast? In the United States the average age of achieving this goal is 54, but there are many who are there by age 45 and a

growing number of much younger entrepreneurs who are claiming the same success. Be specific about where you want to see yourself in three years, five years and ten years. You might even want to think about when you want to retire or how you want to spend those later years.

3. Develop a strategy. Today's most successful young millionaires have made their money by selling a service or a product. Today's millionaires followed outline and proven steps to become a millionaire fast. It is not impossible, but it often takes longer to build your own wealth while working for someone else and helping them build theirs.

4. Start with a project that you can manage. Build your self-esteem while you build your reputation. Just work harder than anyone else in your field. A strong work ethic is a common factor in becoming a financial superstar. Find ways to differentiate your service or product and market, market, market it.

5. Learn from others. Don't be afraid to study other successful business models and imitate what works. Why waste time re-inventing the wheel when you can benefit from what is already working? Surround yourself with like-minded energetic, positive entrepreneurs but keep your thoughts independent as you follow your own path to success.

6. Manage the money you now have by:
Paying off outstanding debts as quickly as possible. Living below your means so that you can save and invest.
Setting aside an emergency fund for unexpected bumps in the road.

Learning to delay gratification by making decisions that support your long term goals.

Getting sound financial/business advice from experts as needed.

Serious About Learning How to Become a Millionaire? 7 Inside Secrets to Quickly Help You Get There!

Secret #1 ... Perception, it's not necessarily what something really is but more about how you perceive what it is. Here's what I mean. A person with no money looks at an opportunity and thinks, "How much is this going to cost me?" A person who has learned how to think correctly looks at an opportunity and thinks, "How much can I make from this opportunity?" That subtle difference is what truly separates the rich from the poor. How is your - perception?

Secret #2 ... Product, it does not have to be from selling your own product. Most people think you have to come up with some great invention. When the truth of the matter is, most people who have learned how to become a millionaire have just found a product that sells like crazy and then they sell it over and over and over again.

Secret #3 ... Ideas, a lot of people think that you have to be a great thinker and come up with a terrific idea. The truth is most people who have made their millions have taken an idea that already existed and with a small tweak turned it into millions.

Secret #4 ... Perfection, it is harder to become a millionaire if you are a perfectionist. People who are perfectionists spend all of their time trying to get something perfect before bringing it to the market place. People who know how to become a millionaire know that they just have to get going, and they'll take care of perfecting their product or service as they go along.

Secret #5 ... Excuses, maybe you have heard you can make excuses or you can make money but you can't make both. Nothing holds truer if you are looking at learning how to become a millionaire. People who tough it out years and years at a job they hate make excuses. People who make millions make no excuses no matter what the economy is like or what is on the evening news.

Secret #6 ... When is the best time for making your millions? There are more millionaires made during bad economic times then at any other time. Timing could not be any better than in today's economy. The time for you to learn how to become a millionaire could be right around the very next corner.

Secret #7 ... The sky is falling, the sky has been here for millions and millions of years and is going nowhere. If you think it's doom and gloom, then it is. If you think it is bright and the sun is shining, then it is. If you think it's hard to learn how to become a millionaire, then it is. If you think it is easy to learn how to become a millionaire, then it is.

How to Become a Millionaire - 14 Tips to Help Anyone Succeed (Regardless of Your Situation)

The best way to become a millionaire is to make a decision to become one and stick it out until it happens no matter how long it may take you. If you ask most people if they would like to have a million dollars, most of them will tell you yes. However, most people may really like to have a million dollars but will not pay the price to become a millionaire. Sure it may be possible to make a million by winning it in a lottery but the odds are really stacked against you in the long run. Millions of people play the lottery regularly in hopes of striking it rich but only do so because the upfront cost of the ticket is relatively cheap and it takes absolutely no effort at all to purchase one.

If someone actually wins the lottery (and most will not), they still have to deal with a common problem. Most people who become a millionaire by winning it do not keep it for very long. Many lose their money and end up broke within a few years. This happens because most people truly can't handle money. Yes you may be one of the few who can but most people can not handle more than they are used to earning per year. Most people are not taught how to raise their financial IQ's in school. They teach you how to establish a good career and become a good employee in school. School does not teach you how to become financially wealthy. Now back to the lottery topic. If you were actually one of the few who won a million, and ever lost it, most likely you will not know how to create another million again. On the other hand, if you made it and lost it for any reason, most likely you will be able to make another million. Donald Trump made billions of dollars. Later things took a down turn and he lost everything. Within a year he was able to make it all back. Once your mind learns how to make a million, it can always create it again.

Here are 14 tips to help you become a millionaire:

1. Your Why: What is your reason for making this kind of money? Have you had a life long dream of achieving something, living some way or have you gone though a lot of pain in the past as a direct result of lack of funds? If your why is big enough and strong enough, you will make it. If they aren't, you will not. Use any pain or grief that has been bottled up inside you for years. This will be your fuel.

2. Passion: Come up with a money making idea that you are passionate about. If you are passionate about it, then it will not be work and it will give you pleasure building it. If it gives joy in the growth periods, things will move along at a faster pace for you and prosperity will come a lot quicker.

3. Don't Quit Your Day Job: Keeping your job will allow you to leverage the income that you are already earning. You must keep earning what you are earning right now in order to keep the financial strain off your shoulders while you build extra wealth in your spare time. You can not attract more money if you are under strain.

4. Passive Income: Look for ways to increase your income by leveraging passive income streams. Passive income is an income stream that keeps growing without your constant work and effort or direct supervision. Examples of passive income are: real estate, Laundromats and Stocks and Bonds. Try to be creative in finding ways to make passive income.

5. Live Within Your Means: Yes you will still have to learn how to remain conservative even while making your first million. You must first learn how

to keep and then grow your money. You may have a taste for exotic or finer things in life but you will have to put a cap on your spending for now. Put off buying that sports car or buying that dream home for now. Most people first buy the car and home then end up being trapped paying for these things for the rest of their lives.

6. Learn How to Budget: Make your hard earned money last longer and go farther. Cut off spending on things that you really do not need right now. Prosperity will not come if you do not make the best of what you already have. This is one of the laws of the universe.

7. Appreciation: Learn to appreciate everything that God has already given you in life. Thank God for everything that you have especially if you never gave thanks for receiving them before. If you do not appreciate what you already have, it will be hard for you to receive any more.

8. Set a Deadline: Set a date when you expect to receive your first million dollars. This is very important. This date must be something that your conscious mind can believe. Once a deadline has been set, the work (action) will expand to create the money by that time. This is another phenomenon.

9. Overcome Obstacles: Once you make any commitment especially something as big as making your first million, there will be Goliaths in your path. Basically, once anyone makes a big commitment to themselves, they will be tested. Just keep steering towards your road blocks and you will eventually find a way around them or even through them. These road blocks are just put in your path as a test

to see if you really want what you asked for. Most people will quit at the sign of the first road block. Do not make this mistake. If you really want it, you can overcome obstacles and receive the fruits of your labors.

10. Patience: It may take sometime for your first million to be made or manifest. You must learn how to become patient as it is well worth the wait. The amount of time it takes is different for everyone.

11. Perseverance: There will be days that you will want to quit and pack it in. This is the biggest mistake that you could ever make. Most people quit just before they actually make it.

12. Faith: You must have faith that you will achieve your goal. No one is denied what they have asked for if they truly believe that they can actually get it. Know that creating your first million is possible especially since millions of people have done it before (According to the research made by CapGemini and Merryl Lynch published in the World Wealth Report in 2006, there are 8.7 plus million millionaires throughout the world).

13. Model Wealthy People: Read biographies of the rich and famous and learn what they went through to make their first millions. Learn how they went around their obstacles and how they dealt with pressure.

14. Personal Development: Take some time everyday to build yourself internally. You must grow from the inside before your prosperity can grow on your outside.

This concludes my 14 tips to assist you in learning how to become a millionaire. It may seem like a very big undertaking and most people will quit long before they earn or manifest their first million. That doesn't have to happen to you if you stick with it and believe in yourself. No matter what limitations you may think you have right now, you can overcome them. Imagine what your life will be like if you do.

How to Become a Millionaire - 8 Truths

I was inspired to write this article when I read Keith Cameron Smith's Book "The 10 Distinctions Between Millionaires and the Middle Class". The book resonated with my ideas so well that I almost could've written the book. I have taken some of his ideas, meshed it with my own to create this short article on How To Become a Millionaire.

1. Millionaires think long-term. I've long believed that the difference between successful people and unsuccessful people has to do with the ability for delayed gratification. If you think about those people in society whom are respected and successful - they often have a lot of education, which means they delayed making money and worked hard; they delayed gratification. This is also true of great sports figures or Olympic athletes, they spend hours working out and practicing their craft instead of sitting in front of the television.
2. Embrace change. We all wish for the good old days, but the fact is the good old days will never happen again, change is opportunity. Accept it, prepare for it, study for it and you will thrive.

It's not survival of the fittest, it's survival of the most adaptable and our world changes rapidly, the more we can adapt, the better we can do.

3. Be a constant learner. I've even gone so far as to not have a television. Instead I read, I believe it feeds my mind more. I believe in being a constant learner, I ask myself everyday before I go to bed "what did I learn today?".

   I also choose topics I feel I need to know more about and I study them. That's the habit of Millionaires.

4. Ask empowering questions. In most cases, empowering questions are how. How can I do this or how can I do that, as opposed to why. If you ask why, you often get the reason and it reinforces an unsuccessful loop.

   Asking a big how question also inspires greater action than a small how question. How can you increase sales by 6% comes back with almost no changes to doing things the same way. How can you increase sales 50% creates a change that you'll need to do something dramatically different.

5. Be frugal. Now I don't mean cheap - I mean frugal. Frugal is about getting good value for money, so I'm often willing to spend a higher price if I feel the value I'm receiving is better value.

6. Start now. I've found that life is much easier for me because I started hard and worked hard from a very young age. That created a momentum effect that has now made my life much easier.

7. Be grateful. I'm a big believer in having an attitude of gratitude. I know I lead a charmed life and I appreciate everything in life.

8. Be giving. To not be generous with both time and money creates the lack of abundance and a fear there is limited resources. Being generous creates the opposite effect.

   For myself, the toughest one is time, since I am a time management guy and my time is so valuable.

9. Study time management. I'm a big believer that most of my success has to do with using my time well, which is largely having proper goals, knowing what needs to be done and then setting my priorities.

How To Become A Millionaire: Living Below Your Means

Sure, you probably won't be super rich and driving a super car anytime soon while pulling in twenty thousand dollars a year. That isn't to say that you can never become wealthy. There are however several key factors to building wealth that will surely determine your abilities to succeed. The most important, and unfortunately the most ignored principle people face is that of living below their means. The biggest problems I believe tend to be psychological. The first issue being that of the get it now, pay for it later mindset.

Credit Card Debt Can Destroy You

Most difficult of all, is maintaining and using credit cards properly. The average person can't, not for the lack of trying, it is just extremely difficult to resist purchasing something you believe that you need now, and expecting to pay for it later. Knowing all to well the perils of credit cards, I purposefully leave mine at home. Now when an apparent need for them arise, I would have to go back home, and get them. Usually by that time, I have reconsidered the need for whatever it was that I wanted in the first place. However, if your not consistently renting vehicles, or staying at motels, you should reconsider even having them.

No matter the emergency, if you've reached a point that you need a credit card to bail you out, consider that if you make a purchase with it and pay for it with your next pay check, it is very likely that you'll end up in the same situation again since your next pay check will be taking an unexpected hit. This can, and often does lead to a cycle that is extremely difficult to break from, especially for those that are living pay check to pay check. It's often better to admit defeat, and find an alternative rather than making that purchase on a credit card.

If you choose to keep, and make use of your credit cards, you've got to be extremely disciplined in their usage, and always sleep on a financial decision. It is all to easy to justify a temptation and fall prey to the idea of instant gratification. Instead, wait a full day and decide if you truly need it, or if you could do without it. If you would truly like it, come up with a savings plan for it. Earning something by working hard to fight temptation, and saving over time is so much more gratifying.

Reducing Your Cost Of Living

Reductions of cost is often much more effective than complete elimination. For example, instead of deciding to for example get rid of your cell phone, figure out what features you absolutely need, and which you could do without, then call your provider and get those features removed, and ask them if they can provide a better deal on those features that you do need. You'll find more often than not, that your provider is more than glad to give you a deal, you've just got to be willing to ask for it.

Of course, eliminating an expense completely does offer its own benefits, however it can lead to future over indulgence which can cost more than having it did in the first place. For example, if you're a coffee drinker, it is probably best to continue drinking coffee, but at a reduced rate. Quitting completely can just lead to you falling back on it, and end up drinking and spending more than you ever did before. So be completely sure you can do without something before getting rid of it completely, and test it out. If you think you can do without a cell phone, then take it and toss it in a drawer, and see how you feel in a week. If you found yourself taking it with you, or constantly checking it, then you'd be better off finding features you could reduce, and trying to get a better deal from your provider rather than getting rid of it.

One major expense that many people have is power and fuel, and we use it with such disregard. It takes some getting used to, but you can make it habitual to turn your car off when idling, or shut the lights off when you leave a room. After a week or so it'll become second nature to think about shutting down things that are not in use before you leave. Another thing to do is before purchasing big ticket items like washers, dryers, freezers, stoves, microwaves, and the like is to make your decision based on its energy efficiency rating, and what you truly need.

There are many things you can do in your own home to reduce your cost of living, so take a look around and make it a game to try and reduce your utility usage as much as possible, not only does it help your budget, but it helps the environment as well.

Conclusion

Reducing your credit card dependencies, and cost of living can help you live below your means, but don't limit yourself. Always be looking for new ways to save money, whether it be brewing your own coffee, or switching to cold water detergent. There are a lot of cheaper alternatives, and methods to decrease your costs. So long as you open your eyes to them.

CHAPTER 5

Placement Programs Private and Trade Platforms - What They Really Are

Trading Platforms are pools of capital that invest in a wide variety of financial instruments including stocks, bonds, commodities, ETF's and foreign exchange. These pools of capital may be a number of legal entities; however, the most common is known as a PPP, an acronym for Private Placement Programs. Private Placement Trading Programs are not offered to the general public. They are exactly what their name implies, offerings of membership interest to a select group of chosen investors who meet certain financial requirements.

The minimum investment in these Private Placement Programs can often be quite high and require a lockup period, where the capital is committed to the Trade Program for a certain amount of time. The minimum investment levels and principal commitment periods vary depending on the type of investments and the objective of the investment. One year lock ups are not uncommon and in some investments the lock up period may be even longer. Lock ups serve a very important function. They provide the Trade Platform Managers and Platform Traders with time in which to obtain results for the investors. Platform Traders want to know that the capital allocations they have been given to trade are for a long enough period of time to allow a particular trading strategy time to mature.

If you were to look at the returns of outstanding Platform Traders you would see profitable results over time; however, in the short term they may have a period of negative returns. If your interest is in traders with no down periods, please read no further, as they do not exist, contrary to popular belief. There is no such thing as free money. Trading involves risk. Every investor dreams of opening the door today and finding tomorrows Wall Street Journal, but this only exists in fantasy. Platform Trading requires hard work, tremendous discipline, patience and superb talent. The fact is very few people have the gifts to be a successful trader. The Platform Traders at the very top of their peers are rewarded with staggering wealth. Platform

Traders utilize many strategies to help determine profitable trades, such as macro analysis, price theory, fundamental analysis, value analysis and many more investment strategies. What superior and outstanding Platform Traders can do is make enough winning trades over time, irrespective of what strategy they may use to accumulate trading profits. However, a number of their trades will not be winners. A large part of successful Private Placement Program trading is risk management; controlling losses and preserving investment capital.

One of the very basic risk management techniques utilized by Private Placement Program Traders is only risking a very small percentage of the investment capital on every trade. It is usually between one half and two percent on a particular trade. If a trade loss hits a defined percentage allocation, the trade is closed out. The average investor has an extremely difficult time taking a loss. In fact, it is a human tendency to hold on to losing trades and cut winning trades short, which is the very opposite of what great Platform Traders do. Risk management systems can get very complex and Platform Traders often write complex algorithms to manage risk when there are many positions and trade strategies running all at once.

The advent of the computer has radically revolutionized trading, just as it has every facet of our lives. Modern Trading Platforms are heavily dependent on mathematics and the hard sciences. Most Platform Traders today have advances formal education and training in mathematics, probabilities, physics, computer science, economics and engineering. Trade rooms are more similar to busy computer driven laboratories than the old image of guys in a boiler- room shouting into two telephones at one time. Almost all orders are input electronically and trades are matched up by sophisticated software. Private Placement Programmers and software engineers are indispensable to successful Private Placement Programs and Trade Platforms.

As mentioned earlier, Platform Traders have many products to trade and a huge number of global exchanges to execute the trades. The most well-known exchange in the world is the New York Stock Exchange (NYSE). When Platform Traders make a trade, that trade is executed on an exchange. The NYSE, CME, NYMEX, ICE, CBOE and NASDAQ are the largest U.S. exchanges. In Europe the LSE, Euronext and Frankfort Exchange are largest. In commodities much of the execution is done on the Globex, an electronic exchange. Platform Traders use the exchanges to buy and sell trillions of dollars of stocks, bonds, currencies, gold, oil, euro-dollars, CMO's, ETF's and hundreds of other securities, currencies and derivatives in efforts to make profits for themselves and investors.

Private Placement Program Traders can make profits by buying a particular instrument or by shorting, (selling it) betting the price will go down. Some Platform Traders buy and sell similar instruments simultaneous, betting on the change in price between the two instruments; this is called arbitrage and spread trading. Other Platform Traders employ option strategies, such as writing options, writing straddles, strangles, butterflies and condors. Option strategies can quickly become extremely complex and are a highly specialized area of trading which requires extraordinary expertise.

Private Placement Trading Platforms utilize margin to buy and sell all of the various instruments they trade. Margin is simply a partial payment for the instrument. Most people are familiar with margin on stocks. Margins are met with cash, period. Contrary to what some people may believe, the only instrument that is good for backing a trade position is cash. When a profit is made, it is credited to the Trade Platforms books that day; when a loss is taken it is debited from the Trade Platforms books that day. Private Placement Platform Trading is a cash business; gains and losses are marked to market each day. Trade Platform Managers should know by between midnight and two a.m.

each trading day where they stand. The Private Placement Trade Platforms maintain what is called a customer segregated account with an FCM. This account is where the Trade Platform Investors' funds are held. An independent capital account is established for each Trade Platform Investor in order to provide accurate accounting on a monthly or quarterly basis. The Private Placement Platforms' funds are deposited into a master segregated funds account to be used for margin in trading.

Goldman Sachs, Merrill Lynch, ABN AMRO, MF Global, JP Morgan Chase, Credit Suisse, Deutsche Bank and Bank of America are all FCMs. These companies, as well as handling trades for independent Trade Platforms for many years, have had their own internal proprietary trading desk or Trade Platforms. Some of these trade desks are famous such as Goldman's Alpha Fund, Morgan Stanley's PDT (Process Driven Trading) Platform and Deutsche Bank's legendary SABA Trading Program, led by Boaz Weinstein. The new regulatory environment is forcing many of the banks to divest themselves of proprietary Trading Platforms. This is making for a large talent pool comprising the best and brightest traders available for Private Placement Programs, Private Hedge Funds and Trading Platforms.

Private Placement Programs and Trading Platforms often use what is known as notionalization or notional funding to increase the leverage that the Trade Platform may use. The Trading Platforms may leverage its trading capital as much as ten times, meaning that One Hundred Million Dollars ($100,000,000) may be traded as it was a Billion Dollars ($1,000,000,000).

Leverage, while giving the ability to greatly increase the returns on cash can also lead to significant loss. The old adage that "leverage is a double-edge sword" is very true. Notionalization absolutely must be constantly monitored and adjusted, depending on margin requirements and market conditions. The Private Placement Platform Managers have investment committees that are responsible for determining notional trading levels. Notionalization is a very powerful tool for the Private Placement Trading Platforms.

In conclusion, when it comes to Private Placement Programs, the minimum investment can be high and the risk can be high as well. However, the reward can be great, great enough to easily justify the investment and risk for one who has the means with which to get involved in such an investment.

Large Debt Instruments Market for Private Placement Programs

There is a tremendous daily market of discounted bank instruments like SBLC, Bonds, MTN, BG, etc. involving issuing banks and long chains of what are called "exit-buyers", which include huge financial institutions, Pension Funds, etc. in an exclusive Private Placement Program arena.

These activities on the bank side are done as "Off- Balance Sheet Activities", which allow the banks to benefit in many ways. So, what are "Off-Balance Sheet Activities"? Basically, they are contingent liabilities and assets, where the value depends upon the outcome upon which the claim is based, similar to that of an option. These "Off-Balance Sheet

Activities" show up on the balance sheet merely as memoranda items. When they cause a cash flow, they will show up as a debit or credit on the balance sheet. Since there is no deposit liability, the bank does not have to consider binding capital constraints.

So, what is the difference between private placement programs and normal trading?

Since all Private Placement Programs involve trading with discounted debt instruments (notes) and can only be done on a private level in order to bypass legal restrictions, these types of trades are different from the highly regulated "normal" trading. Said another way, these Private Placement Programs are done and restricted on a private level only without all of the restrictions that are present in the securities market.

What is "normal trading"? It is what the majority of the public is aware of and is known as the open market (or spot market) under which bids and offers are used to buy and sell discounted instruments. Kind of like an auction.

To play here the traders must have full control of the funds, if they don't, they cannot buy the instruments and sell them to others. Also, there are no arbitrage buy-sell transactions in this market because all players have a clear view of the instrument and its price.

There is also something called a "closed, private market" where an inner circle exists and is made up of a restricted number of "master commitment holders".

These are basically trusts with large amounts of money that agree (through contracts) to purchase a specified number of fresh-cut instruments at a set price during a set period of time. Their purpose is to sell these fresh- cut instruments on, so they contract sub-commitment holders, who contract with exit-buyers they find.

Because all of these programs all based on arbitrage buy-sell transactions with preset prices, the traders do not have to be in control of the investor's funds. But in order for a program to start, there has to be enough money behind each buy-sell transaction. That's why the investors are needed. The involved banks and commitment holders are not permitted to trade with their own money unless they have reserved enough funds on the market, and that money belongs to the investors which is never used, and never put at risk.

These Trading Banks can lend out money to the "traders" usually at 1: 10 ratio, but under certain conditions, they go as high as 20: 1. That means that if a trader can "reserve" $iooM, then the bank can lend out $1 Billion. This is accomplished through a line of credit based on how much money the trader (the commitment holder) has, since the banks don't lend out that much money without collateral.

Any trader that requires he be in control of the investor's fund, is not one of the major players, but rather plays in the open spot market where lots of different instruments are traded.

Now if the trader only has to reserve the client's funds without being in control of those funds, he is participating in this private market of private placement programs.

Since many bankers and others in the financial arena are exposed to the open market but are not allowed into the private market, they find it difficult to believe that a private market exists and that is often the reason they think private placement programs are scams.

What Is A Private Placement Program And How Do You Avoid Fraudsters

What is a private placement program (PPP)? PPP refers to non-public securities that are usually sold to a few private investors. In the US, these placements are subject to the Securities Act but they are not subject to registration with the SEC (Securities and Exchange Commission) as long as issuance conforms to the regulations of the Securities Act of 1933.

Most PPPs are offered in terms of the rules of Regulation D. A private placement typically consists of shares, stocks (common or preferred), promissory notes, warrants, and other forms of membership interests. Buyers are often institutional investors like pension funds, insurance companies, and banks.

Right now, the number of people seeking PPPs is higher than ever. Even though this is a small niche market, every month about 3,000 people are asking internet search engines to find Private Placement

Programs. This being the case, PPP business has unfortunately become infested with fraudsters. With this in mind, here are some cautionary tips for prospective clients.

Do not deal with broker chains in a PPP transaction. No more than four brokers should be involved in a deal (including the client's representative and the program manager). This can result in greed and severely distorted information.

Only deal with traders or brokers who have closed previous transactions. Although there are thousands out there claiming to have PP connections, most of them have never closed deals. They may even have been working for years and years with no success. This is a clear sign that nothing is going to change. When you first speak to someone, ask quite aggressively if he or she has been paid. The tone and response will indicate if the truth is being told or not. Use this and their level of intellect as a guide.

If you are told that someone famous is attached to the deal, insist on speaking with this person to make sure you are not wasting your time. There are some well- known figures who are involved in PPPs but, if you come across a name-dropper, be dubious and demand to speak with him or her. You may well be onto a good thing if they can prove they are involved in the deal. Nevertheless, bear in mind that there are only a few hundred people in the entire world who are connected to genuine private placement programs.

Always establish relationships on the telephone or face-to-face on Skype. Never use email. There is no way that a person who is serious about business and has closed a transaction would agree to primarily communicate through email. Someone who is successful, values their time, and has nothing to hide, would much rather get the deal done quickly via Skype.

The only way to form trustworthy relationships in this game is on Skype or over the telephone because people can assess your demeanor, tone, and knowledge. Email has little effect because it only allows written communication. The information in this article should have provided some answers to the question - What is a private placement program? If you are serious about getting into this business, you are going to have to be assertive and aggressive.

Private Placement Program: The Process of PPP Trade Brief on the private placement program:

The private placement program / PPP trade is a money intensive program which requires high funding potentials. This program has been designed as a high investment trade where the profit margin is immense. The basic requirement to ply this trade is the ability to arrange for valid financial credits / asset valuation and risk management skills.

The application process:

Primarily a private investor is needed to complete the application process with appropriate documentation that validates his/her financial assests. Other paper documents include identity card, residential proofs, proofs for nationality and other essential information that qualifies a person as a living entity.

Importance of asset evaluation:

Amongst all the documents the asset evaluation plays an important part. It is based on this credential that an investor is granted or declined the proposal of private placement program or private trading. When considered for such a program the license issuing board pays considerable importance to the fact whether the assets are of floating or fixed origin. The fixed assets are the non-cash types, meaning that they cannot be adequately utilised while plying the private trade program. This may include types of personal bonds or other financial instruments that has been extended in an incorrect manner.

The verification part:

After the successful completion of the application process it now depends on the authorized board to meticulously speculate the financial strength of the client and judge whether he/she is capable of carrying out the requisites in a proper way. Verification of the submitted documents and their legitimacy also accounts for the sanction of the private trading license. In most cases it has been noted that the viable clients who are granted the opportunity of this profitable trade are the corporate houses. However if private investors can suffice the required capital then their proposal may also stand the chance of being considered (subject to specifications).

One thing that is to be kept in mind while filing for application is that, the proposal for Private placement program license can be kept pending for weeks. The most suitable entrepreneur is given the first preference while others have to keep their patience and wait for their chance. Thus the private placement program it can be concluded is not meant for every entrepreneur who wants to engage in lucrative business trade. Until and unless one gets a license for the concerned authority he/she cannot take to the merchandise of PPP trade instruments.

Raise Capital With Private Placement Programs and Platforms - PPM For Any Business Or Start Up

Times are changing in the world of business finance. No longer are commercial bank loans the only way to finance a business. In today's modern business environment any entrepreneur can raise capital with private placement programs and platforms. Private capital is available to any entrepreneur with any size of business, small, medium or large.

The most widely used platform is provided by the United States Securities and Exchange Commission (SEC). The SEC has set in place a set of rules and regulations that provide an exemption from the expensive registration process for companies who need to sell stock shares to raise capital from private investors. The most popular of these Regulations is known as Regulation D, which contains Rules 504, 505 and 506.

Although many small business owners are aware of private capital few have the resources to locate private investors, and few possess the upfront capital to pay professionals the required fees to design and develop the investment documents. Developing an investment offering typically requires an attorney, and/or other professionals, who specialize in private placements. Everyone knows that most entrepreneurs have limited capital when starting a business. Prior to 2002 private capital was extremely expensive. The capital itself was not necessarily the most expensive item, but the preparation costs were over-the-top expensive. Entrepreneurs needed a selling document that was vetted by legal experts and/or consultants. This selling document is called the PPM or Private Placement Memorandum. The PPM provides details for every aspect of the business and the investment being sought.

In the earlier days Private Placement Memorandum development started at $15,000 and went as high as $50,000. These prices are still found today in more specialized areas such as Hedge Funds and public offerings, however, a few savvy entrepreneurs have narrowed this price margin substantially over the last 8- 9 years bringing the prices down to roughly $4,500 through online services.

Nearly all companies qualify for Regulation D: Any Business or Start Up, Hedge Funds, Large Public Corporations, Mid-Sized Companies, Foreign Corporations, you name it. Literally any type of company can qualify for a Regulation D Private Placement.

The prerequisites include, but are not limited to:

1. A selling document (PPM)
2. A Form D Filing at the SEC (no filing fee)
3. A State Filing in whatever state the company raises private capital (small filing fee)
4. No soliciting to investors
5. The securities are sold as restricted from transfer or trading for 12 months
6. The amounts of capital raised must adhere to one of the Regulation D Rules, e.g., 504, 505, 506

Throughout the history of business cycles in the United States the typical avenue for business financing has required long bank applications, expensive business plans, or SBA involvement.

Investing in Private Placement Trading Programs - Is It For You?

Private placement trading programs are the opposite of public investments. Unlike public investing opportunities, only a small number of qualified people will be invited to invest privately in a company's business interests. From there, investing in private placement trading programs results in a profit for investors. The private transaction typically takes place between two parties and a middle facilitator. When it comes to all the investment opportunities that exist, this is truly one of the most lucrative options available to you. This kind of trading is based on the fractional reserve banking system, which is not a difficult concept to understand once you learn how it is tied to this kind of investing.

Once you have a clear understanding of what investing in these kid of programs involves and how fractional reserve banking comes into play, you must discover a way to get into a trading platform. This step near the beginning of the process can be the most difficult of all. This is because private placement trading is exactly that-private and secret. If you want to get involved with these programs or other alternative investment opportunities, you need to get in touch with an investing and trading company.

Getting started in investing in trading programs can yield huge returns. Placements typically start at more than $1 million and there is no cap as to how much you can invest. With this amount of money you may be given estimates from brokers of unbelievable possibilities in return amounts. It may sound too good to be true, and it probably is. To keep yourself from becoming greedy, you need to keep a realistic view on your investment and potential returns. Some opportunities may indeed yield incredible returns because this is a lucrative investment opportunity, but others many not meet up to your expectations. This is simply the nature of investing in private placement trading programs.

The best way to make money with trading programs is to find a genuine opportunity. The last thing you want, after all, is to be strung into a deal that ends up being illegal or illegitimate in some way. To spot an opportunity that you want to avoid, see if national brokerage firms refuse to become involved in the private placement program. When this happens, it may be the case that the brokerage firm has been bitten when investing in private placement trading programs before and they want to avoid a repeat occurrence.

Private Placements Are Sometimes Bad Investments

A Private Placement Trading Program (PPP) is a lucrative way of investing and as long as the PPP is genuine, there is no financial risk for investors. As you can imagine, if you are offered a no-risk high profit opportunity in the stock market business you would probably be tempted to jump at the chance. However if you are tempted by PPPs beware, and realize that they are not always what they seem. Many investors have been stung in PPP scams and billions of dollars have been lost. There are law suits underway, but they are notoriously slow to reach a conclusion and given the amount of scams that have been uncovered, relatively few perpetrators have gone to court.

High Returns for Ethical Investments

Private Placement Programs are those trading with Medium term Bank Notes (MTNs) or Treasury bills (T-

Bills). They typically have a high return on the investment and are, more often than not associated with ethical trading. They involve programs which are humanitarian in nature. Investors are required to put part of their earnings into projects which are concerned with humanitarian, social or economic development. Profits from such projects go back into the economy, giving it a much needed boost.

It is Not Legal for Financial Institutions to Invest in PPPs

Financial Institutions are not legally allowed to participate in such programs so have to find private individuals or companies to invest in them. The investor cannot lose money as the investment is underwritten by the trading group.

This means that the investor is in a win-win situation for once, so it is hardly surprising that some unethical companies have found PPPs useful for conning high level investors out of their capital. The difficulty is that every investor would love to invest in a PPP, but can't access them as they open and close quickly, so it is very difficult to find a performing trade.

Tell-Tale Signs That All is Not Well

When national brokerage firms refuse to touch Private Placement Programs, it's a sure sign that something is "rotten in the state of Denmark" to quote Shakespeare. Even with high commissions available and fees, PPPs are considered dangerous. It's a case of once bitten twice shy. Businesses have invested unethically in fields that they are not allowed to invest in under the terms of PPPs, including pornographic web sites. So now brokers are very wary of even considering a PPP.

Basically, as with every other promise of spectacular wealth or extravagant claims of what product X can do for you, the reality is that the investment or product really is too good to be true. Unfortunately, PPPs are to be looked into very carefully. If you do get a genuine one, then you can count yourself extremely lucky.

Write Your Own Private Placement and Save Thousands

If you are reading this then you are probably aware opinions vary as to the effectiveness of Private Placement Memorandum templates. Some "experts" will lead you to believe you are much better off spending upwards of $18,000 to have a securities attorney prepare your entire Memorandum. Our experience tells a very different story.

Private Placements are an approved form of documentation for raising capital under Regulation D. The Regulation D programs were designed to provide an exemption to sell securities in a private capital raise without registering the securities. The process of securities registration is complex, time consuming and expensive. Without the Regulation D exemption, many businesses would not have a viable option for raising capital.

The PPM document makes it much easier and less expensive for private companies to access funding and raise capital. However, creating a Memorandum from scratch is near impossible. PPMs are long, complex legal documents and you simply cannot know what needs to be included if you haven't done it before.

This is why templates are useful, the complex framework has already been organized and written for you. All you need to do is download the template and then follow instructions to easily customize for your business.

High quality templates are the product of real experience raising real capital, while providing full protection under the Regulation D exemptions.

Templates do not seek to displace the legal profession - attorneys provide valuable services. On the contrary, in order to ensure your Private Placement complies with federal and state regulations businesses you should seek a legal review of their completed PPM before soliciting investors.

However, by first completing the draft PPM yourself, and then seeking a qualified attorney review, you can dramatically reduce your costs. Our clients report saving $17,000 or more compared to having the attorney complete the entire PPM.

Using our proven templates, you can customize your own Private Placement for a fraction of the time and cost because the hard work has been done for you.

High-quality templates will improve your chances to win funding.

Bottom line, do not spend thousands up-front before you ever raise a dime.

Elevate Ventures provides capital formation and consulting services to entrepreneurial stage and emerging growth companies.

Private Placement Investments Secrets

What Trump & Buffet won't tell you: "How to Maximize your Return & Eliminate Risk"

There are many things in life that are kept hidden from common public knowledge for one reason or another, but ultimately they are there if you do some research and find them. The number one thing that is not readily known is that there are "retail investments" and "wholesale investments". The majority of the public only knows about "retail investments". The character of retail investments are lower returns and sometimes even higher risk. The reason that some of these retail investments are higher risk is that they shed off so little return that you are actually losing money when you compute inflation into the equation. The reason that they give you such little return is that they say your principle is safe. Ask yourself this question: "How safe is my money, when it is actually losing money consistently when inflation is taken into account"? Another question to ask is "How much of my principle is at risk"? Let's take a look at just some of the many "retail investments".

1. Stocks
2. Mutual Funds
3. CD's (Credit Deposits)
4. T-Bills and T-Bonds

Now the question should be what are "wholesale investments"? Wholesale investments in and of themselves are highly protected in nature. The reason the previous statement is true is because the majority of the wholesale investments are private or "by invitation only". They are peer to peer or small groups of networks. You have to know someone who has access to the wholesale investments in order for you to have access to them. There are various reasons for this. One, of many, is that there are a lot of regulations that are placed on investments deemed "public worthy" by the SEC and various other regulatory agencies. These are your retail investments that everyone knows about. The people that have access to the desired wholesale investments have no desire to put up with regulatory agencies and to be honest, don't have the time. The regulatory agencies are fine with these wholesale investments operating, just as long as the people running these types of investments don't advertize or solicit for business. So these are the rules that everyone plays by. Everyone is happy, except for the general public which is not given the full picture of all of the different types of investment vehicles which are available. The characteristics of wholesale investments is high rates of return, paid weekly, monthly, and sometimes yearly depending on what the investment is and are by invitation only. Most of these wholesale investments have very little risk and the best ones have zero risk. That is right, let me repeat myself, the best wholesale investments eliminate risk. Really, the only downside to these wholesale investments is that there are mandatory minimum investment amounts. Generally speaking, $1ook USD is the minimum. The majority of wholesale investments source the funds as well. This is for the protection of everyone involved. Let's take a look at some of the different types of wholesale investments that are out there:

1. Private Placement Memorandums- Allows you to invest in a private company before they go public on a stock exchange by doing an IPO (Initial Public Offering).
2. Corporate Investment Programs- Consist of contracting with financial institutions. Everything from returns to funds placement is contracted. This particular investment is one of the best wholesale investments available. There are two reasons this is the case. It has an extremely high rate of return and risk is eliminated due to the contractual component of this type of investment.
3. Private Managed Accounts- These are different than public managed accounts, as they do not advertize and are only available through word of mouth, usually an intermediary.
4. 506 Regulation D- Another form of Private Placement Memorandums
5. Syndications- These types of investments are different almost each and every time they are put together. The main thing to know is that they are temporary in nature and work for a common goal.

Unless you have already invested in some of these, likely you do not have access to them. There are many different ways to get involved with them, but the easiest is to know someone that is already involved with them. Though this might sound like an impossible mission, I can personally tell you it is not. The best and most effective way to do this is to use an intermediary, private placement individual, or referring broker. Many times, all three are one in the same, meaning that they all do the same thing. These are people that have access to these wholesale investments and would be able to get you into them. There are different protocols to follow when getting into these different types of wholesale investments. Standard documents before even discussing any particulars are:

1. Non-Solicitation Agreement- This basically states that you were not solicited and that you will not go out and solicit for business.
2. NCND (Non-Circumvent & Non-Disclosure)- States that you will not go around your intermediary and that you will not disclose the confidential information.

By submitting these documents, it will get you in the door. After that, there are some compliance departments that will look further into your background and make sure that the funds you have available were not made by any illegal activity and that you do not have ties to people with questionable backgrounds. Remember that these investments are reserved for the best of the best and that if you are fortunate enough to be a part of them, you have to abide and play by the rules.

Some cautions to wrap this up. Believe it or not, there are many individuals that say they have access to these wholesale investments but don't. Sticking to the following guidelines will keep your funds safe and out of harm's way.

1. Never wire your funds anywhere! A lot of dishonest intermediaries try to get you to wire funds to them; they then enter into these wholesale investments, and keep the majority of the returns only giving the actual investor a small portion of them. The only exception is for managed funds. Even then, ask for references for the fund, track records, and a contractual guarantee of returns. Any legitimate managed fund should be able to provide this upon request.

2. Have your lawyer review any contracts! A lot of these wholesale investments are contract driven. This is very good as it provides contractual guarantees. With that being said, you need to have an attorney that understands what you are doing and what sort of program you are getting into. Most of the time, nothing is negotiable in these types of investments. It is an all or nothing type of investment. You still should know what you're getting into by having competent legal counsel to lay it out for you. Also, you should only deal with intermediaries that encourage you to do this. At the least, they should not have a problem with it.

With all that being said, I hope that this report was insightful. Remember that the really neat thing about the contract driven investment, which most of the wholesale investments are, is that you have absolutely no risk and no commitment until those contracts are signed. Nobody makes any money until the contracts are reviewed and signed. Anybody trying to get you to do something else, probably does not have your best interested at heart. If you stick to the guidelines above, it will keep you away from most of the dangers associated with dishonest and unethical people that are out there. Just make sure that you understand that there are great investments out there that are not available to the general public. You just have to find the right people that are "in the know" and have access!

Investing in Trading - Investing in Private Placements Whether you have a private business of your own or are thinking more of investing in trading, one way of finding funding is through investing in private placements. This is a type of capital that banks on trading with treasury bills or medium term bank notes, so it is meant to be a more long-term type of investment process with a high rate of return. This can be far safer for the investor than other types of schemes, for a number of reasons. To get started with finding out if this could be a good idea for your small business or personal investment plan, you should first take a look at the benefits.

One reason why those investing in trading might choose to invest in private placements is that it doesn't require putting up any sort of personal resources or collateral to obtain this type of financing. Another benefit is that these types of trading programs often help benefit humanitarian causes. The profits earned from investments go back to projects that help benefit the economy, or are used for non-profits and social development projects. If that is a draw for you, you should find out what type of works are currently underway, to see if this is something that you might be interested in investing in.

Banks and other financial institutions are not allowed to invest in these programs, which many see as a way of leveling the playing field for smaller personal investors. That makes this a very different type of way of investing in trading, and if the banks do wish to participate they will have to use private investors to purchase shares for them. Because the investment is underwritten by the actual trading group, it is difficult to lose money this way.

However, there are large companies out there that have been known to use private placements as a way of luring investors into unsound schemes, so be sure that you know exactly where your money is going to avoid these types of scams. This is the same with any type of investment, as there is always risk involved whether you are investing in trading, real estate, or start up businesses. For many that is part of the thrill. Investing is a way of playing a game and coming out on top with more money than you started, and if you play the game armed with information, chances are you will succeed.

Keys To Private Placement Venture Investing

Key elements to understand about venture investing are:

- Private Placement venture investing can kick-start your retirement fund like no other tool on the planet.
- Private Placement venture investing can trap your money for 3-10 years before you get out those

returns of 5, 10, 40, or 200 times your original investment.

- Or, over that same 3-10 years, just as has happened to certain mutual funds, you can watch its value go to zero with no way to get out.

The best way to make the really big money in venture investing is portfolio investing, just like the venture and investment banks do. Pick one and it is gambling, invest in 10 or 30 and you have a portfolio strategy that can net 30% to 300% or more per year, year after year after year.

A very large percentage of investors have their funds in "safe" stocks, bonds and mutual funds.

- Here is a recent headline, "Wachovia has lost 52% of its value in the last year."
- Or another quote, "I watched my $1 million retirement fund go to zero as Air Canada went bankrupt."

If you want safety there is no better way than FDIC insured savings accounts, certain CDs and US Government Treasuries. In recent times, on a good day these offered rates of 2-6%. Unfortunately, much of this can be well below the rate of inflation. So that "super safe" deposit can actually be losing value every day!

A good way to try private placement venture investing is to invest in fully compliant offerings that are retirement fund compatible. If your funds are in an existing 401K or similar program you can roll all (or part depending on the plan) into a self directed IRA and then use those funds to buy these compliant private offering stocks. This can limit your tax exposure and is just one of many different ways, but one key is to look for fully complaint offerings. This indicates that the management team of the start-up venture is professionally organized and using professional advice.

How much should you invest? That depends on many factors but a simple key is to recognize that all private placements are high risk and you can lose some or all of your money. For expert advice seek out qualified financial advisors and perhaps even other venture investors. A good rule of thumb is much like the recommendation once given concerning buying a yacht, "If you have to ask what it costs to run it, you don't need one." These are high risk to get the high return; no risk means no high return.

- So invest only what you can afford to lose.
- Good rules of thumb I have heard include investing only 10-25% of your assets in these types of investments and use portfolio strategies.

What kind of returns can you expect? First figure that only 1 in 10 will be a winner. Of the remaining 9 maybe 2 will be OK, and the rest total losers. The greatest returns are in the early seed stages where the business is more of a napkin idea. This is the highest risk stage for any company. For example at this stage the stock may be only $0.10. If at the liquidity event of an IPO, an acquisition or a buyout, the price can be, say, $15.00 in year 5. That is 150 times your original investment. If you invested $25,000, the return is $3,750,000. Not bad for money you could have afforded to lose anyway.

What was once the domain of the few wealthy is now open to many others. This is the reason there are so many angel investors and angel investor clubs. While I am no expert, I can follow the path of the experts and learn from them. The biggest kick your retirement plan or your investment pool can get is from a wide portfolio of private placement investments.

I know of some who have 75% of their funds across a large portfolio of companies. These are individuals of high net worth and who enjoy the world of venture investing. You can pace yourself to be either highly involved or fully passive, your choice. The key is to invest in a portfolio across many different industries and build a catalog of companies at various stages. That way it is possible for you have one or two winners hit each year.

Private placement venture investors range in age from the 20's to over 100 years in age. I know a few founders who are in their teens. The only limit is your ability to invest funds you can lose. That is the key. While in the investment you will not be able to get your funds out until the liquidity event.

Conclusion

Understanding stocks and shares is not a difficult job if you don't get too overly technical and just look for the stock market basics. Stocks are nothing more than purchasing a little piece of a business. When owners of a business need to raise money, they have several options. The first is the normal one, borrow money from a lending institution. The second one is to issue bonds. A bond pays a specific interest rate to those that purchase them. There's a date when it comes due and the company pays the loan in full. The third option is to go public with stock.

Most shares investors and traders would move into shares trading or investing after learning some basic charting, usually moving averages and begin to invest, either making some money or losing some in the initial stages. This is of course, inadequate and a bad way for a someone to start off trading in stocks and shares.

A person would want to invest in stocks and shares because he has good positive cash flow but he is assets poor. By trading in stocks and shares, he is seeking a way to increase his wealth by balancing his cash position with a realistic amount of assets that will grow in time to further improve his wealth position.

It is well accepted that to build up personal wealth, you need to save money- put aside the money until it grows into a huge cashpile, or you continue to do this while you are trading, increasing your capital each time you do so along the way.

At the same time, it is wise policy to use other people's money as a leverage- to increase the capital base and to be able to invest more, with the profits paying back the interest incurred by leveraging.

www.ingramcontent.com/pod-product-compliance
Lightning Source LLC
Chambersburg PA
CBHW061205220326
41597CB00015BA/1499